Craig avoids hyper-spiritual language while delving deeply into how we can cooperate with God as he changes us from the inside out. You won't find clichés or simplistic advice; rather, you'll encounter practical and meaningful guidance on how to walk God's path with grace and guts.

Lee Strobel, *New York Times* bestselling author of
The Case for Faith and *The Case for Christ*

Every pastor wants accessible, well-written resources for people who are new—or returning—to the Christian faith. This is the resource you , engaging, and filled with prac- tica to following Jesus, you need to reac the perfect primer to guide you.

w York Times bestselling author of
The Circle Maker, lead pastor of National Community Church

Insightful and practical, *How to Follow Jesus* is a wonderful guide to living a brand-new way. As a seasoned traveler, Craig offers wise coun- sel, inspirational encouragement, and useful advice to assist and bolster seekers on their eternal adventure.

Danielle Strickland, speaker, author, justice advocate

This book really is a practical guide for following Jesus and growing your faith. It uncomplicates the important matters of faith and provides you a road map for an enriched relationship with Christ.

Mark Sanborn, *New York Times* bestselling author of
The Fred Factor and *The Intention Imperative*

Craig has a passion for helping people find faith in Jesus Christ. Through his outstanding leadership of Alpha USA I have experienced his com- mitment to unity across the church and his infectious reliance on the Holy Spirit. Craig addresses a need with this practical, user-friendly resource for people who have recently come to faith in Jesus.

Nicky Gumbel, pioneer of The Alpha Course and
senior pastor, Holy Trinity Brompton

Sometimes we make following Jesus too complicated and complex. We forget the simplicity, the beauty, the wonder of a vibrant relationship with God. Craig Springer paints a rich portrait of Christ that will revive your heart and renew your spirit.

Margaret Feinberg, author of *Taste and See* and host of *The Joycast*

If you are looking for a simple but challenging explanation for apprenticing with Jesus, then you want to read Craig Springer's *How to Follow Jesus*. If you are new on your spiritual journey or feel stuck spiritually, this book is just what you are looking for!

Dave Ferguson, lead pastor, Community Christian Church; lead visionary, NewThing; author of *Hero Maker: Five Essential Practices for Leaders to Multiply Leaders*

Craig Springer is a man who has his hand on the pulse. He's navigated close to every style of church there is and is now a leading voice for the church nationally and internationally. I can't think of a better man to help Christians navigate the various stages of the Christian faith.

Sam Collier, international speaker and host of *A Greater Story* TV and Podcast

My good friend Craig Springer is a born leader, great communicator and lives on the frontlines of life-transformation. He's just the right person to bring us *How to Follow Jesus*. This book flows from the heart of someone who lives what he says. It's a winsome, authentic, down-to-earth guide to help people step into the life-giving rhythms of following Jesus.

Santiago "Jimmy" Mellado, president and CEO, Compassion International

How to Follow Jesus is a trusted guide and an invigorating read; deeply honest, funny, and filled with practical take-aways. Every person of faith or person wrestling with faith should pick up this book and read it once a year and then share with friends, it's that good.

Mandy Arioto, president and CEO, MOPS International

How to
Follow
Jesus

How to Follow Jesus

A Practical Guide for
Growing Your Faith

Craig Springer

ZONDERVAN
REFLECTIVE

ZONDERVAN REFLECTIVE

How to Follow Jesus
Copyright © 2020 by Craig Springer

ISBN 978-0-310-09318-3 (softcover)

ISBN 978-0-310-09322-0 (audio)

ISBN 978-0-310-09320-6 (ebook)

Requests for information should be addressed to:
Zondervan, *3900 Sparks Dr. SE, Grand Rapids, Michigan 49546*

Published in association with The Christopher Ferebee Agency, www.christopherferebee.com.

Cover design: Rick Szuecs Design
Interior design: Denise Froehlich

Printed in the United States of America

19 20 21 22 23 /LSC/ 10 9 8 7 6 5 4 3 2 1

To all those who hunger for more . . .

Acknowledgments

I want to thank Sarah, my wife and the most important person in my life. Your love, support, confidence-when-I-didn't-have-any, and constant I'm-there-with-you-presence helped me and this book at every turn. Thank you to Isaiah and Isabelle, my children. You fill me with joy and inspiration, and you also encouraged me along the way.

Thank you to the people who impacted those very early years of my faith and growth. Without you, I would have been wandering still. Much of what is in this book, I learned from your lives: John and Linda Larson, David and Christina O'Hara, Ann Healing, Jeff Frazier, Van and Laurie Cochrane, and Sheryl Fleisher.

Thank you to all those who helped me throughout this writing process. Thank you to Margaret Feinberg and Jonathan Merritt for being incredible coaches and friends. Your guidance set me on the path of words and kept me moving. Thank you to Jana Burson and Chris Ferebee for your great representation and wisdom. Thank you to Ryan Pazdur, Greg Clouse, Nathan Kroeze, and the rest of the very skilled team at Zondervan. Thank you to Carrie Schwender, Brian Kreps, and Lisa Uidl for your generous read-throughs and smart edits. Thank you to Bethany Stedman for stepping in with grace, insight, and help at just the right time.

I've had pastors and friends over the past decades who have all shaped the content of these pages and the direction of my life. It always takes a tribe. Thank you.

Contents

Foreword

I remember standing in front of the gothic entrance to Yale Law School and swallowing hard. I was intimidated and apprehensive, and a piece of me wanted to turn around and run the other direction. I felt unprepared and unqualified to study at this august institution, where so many Presidents and Supreme Court justices had grown in their understanding of the law. Certainly, this was a place where I didn't truly belong.

Then came the orientation that the school offers for new students. Professors explained how the curriculum works. We got an in-depth tour of the law library. We were given an opportunity to ask questions. We were offered advice from seasoned students on how to study and prepare for our classes. And we were encouraged over and over again by administrators who seemed to genuinely care about our success.

Armed with the wise counsel and encouragement of those who had already experienced life at Yale, the path forward seemed cleared of obstacles. With newfound courage, I plunged into my studies with confidence and vigor. In the end, I was so glad I didn't give in to my insecurities and walk away. Having the help of those who knew the school well—an orientation to this new experience—made all the difference.

What does this have to do with following Jesus? Let me explain. I was an atheist for much of my life. When my wife became a Christian, I began to use my journalism and legal training to systematically investigate whether there was any evidence for the faith.

After nearly two years, I became convinced that Christianity is true, having been validated by the miraculous resurrection of Jesus.

In many ways, my spiritual journey had been a solitary one. I hadn't even let my wife know about my investigation. I pursued the evidence untethered to any relationships with believers. So after I reached my verdict in the case for Christ and prayed to receive him as my Forgiver and Leader, I was stymied. I wasn't sure what to do next. I felt like I was expected to launch a long and arduous trek up a rugged mountain without the benefit of a map. Pursuing the Christian life seemed like such an intimidating endeavor, a quest for purity and perfection that I could never master. I swallowed hard and hoped for the best.

How I wish I had Craig Springer's book *How to Follow Jesus* at the time! What I needed the most was a concise and engaging orientation to the Christian life—and that's precisely what my friend Craig offers in this highly readable and relatable book.

Craig avoids hyper-spiritual language while delving deeply into how we can cooperate with God as he changes us from the inside out. You won't find clichés or simplistic advice; rather, you'll encounter practical and meaningful guidance on how to walk God's path with grace and guts. In short, here's a reliable roadmap to the Christian faith.

Craig writes from his own wealth of experience as a sincere disciple of the Lord. I can attest to his spiritual maturity and commitment—and they show on virtually every page of his book.

Maybe you feel like I did when I came to faith in Christ: that living the Christian life seems like a mountain you're not ready to climb. If so, you've picked up the right book. Will you stumble along the way? Of course, just as Craig and I have over the years, along with every other Christian. Will your path take unexpected twists and turns? Undoubtedly, but that's part of the adventure of Christianity. Will you be grateful that you've had a guide as honest and transparent as Craig? Absolutely!

Jesus didn't call you to merely be a convert. He wants you to be a disciple, a continual learner who thrives and revels in your relationship with the Creator of all. As you turn the page to begin growing in your faith, keep a highlighter handy. You'll need it to capture the gems of wisdom that Craig provides. And keep in mind the words of the apostle Paul to the Christians in Colossae:

> And now, just as you accepted Christ Jesus as your Lord, you must continue to follow him. Let your roots grow down into him, and let your lives be built on him. Then your faith will grow strong in the truth you were taught, and you will overflow with thankfulness.
>
> COLOSSIANS 2:6–7 (NLT)

Lee Strobel, author,
The Case for Christ
and *The Case for Faith*

CHAPTER 0

The Morning After

The day after I became an all-in, brand-new Christian didn't turn out the way I expected. I woke up excited, thinking everything would be different. By the end of the day, I had smoked a bunch of weed with my partying friends, made out with a girl I liked, and had a knock-down-drag-out argument with my parents about bad grades and staying out too late. In other words, my life after meeting Jesus wasn't much different than my mixed-up life before. I was discouraged.

"Uh-oh," I thought, "something is not right!"

I never imagined I'd become a Christian, but when a friend kept inviting me to church, an unexplainable tug inside of me kept saying "yes." And there I was—big surprise to me—praying a salvation prayer and meaning every word of it. I sure felt like I'd given God everything; the moment was real. My assumption was that—*zap*—I'd wake up the next morning and all of me would instantly change, almost like a magic lightning bolt had struck me from heaven. But then it didn't; I wasn't fixed. Did God mess up? Did I?

The pastor said, "If you give your life to Jesus, you will be made new. A new heart, a new life, a new creation!"

I wanted new. I needed new. But I'd already learned a thing or two about my new beginnings from the past—they rarely lasted. They became false starts. You know, my dreams of being an astronaut, learning to speak fluent Spanish, perfecting the half-pipe on a skateboard, and carving out eight-pack abs to impress the ladies didn't exactly pan out.

"Really, Craig? New?" my inner critic pounded me. "You sure this isn't just another phase, an experiment, a viral video of your life that will soon be forgotten? Is this going to be your spiritual one-hit wonder?" Who still sings "Who Let the Dogs Out" anyway? (Except now you are singing it in your head; *who who who who who?*)

I didn't want my new faith to fade into an empty mental exercise of saying "yes" to a new set of beliefs followed by a hypocritical, half-hearted attempt to live out those beliefs.

I knew I wanted to follow Jesus, but I didn't know how.

In the many years since that first day, I've met hundreds of people who are just like me. People who woke up the morning after their conversion or renewed commitment to Christ with a spiritual hangover; people who were found by Christ but felt lost at the same time. They felt overwhelmed by the mountain of new beliefs, intimidated by a new spiritual vocabulary, and unsure of how to move forward through the constructs of modern-day "religion."

Many of the books I picked up felt heady and impossible or legalistic and impractical. I didn't need to become an expert in church history or theology, and I certainly didn't want to become an insensitive bigot or an un-relatable fanatic. I just wanted to know and follow Jesus in a realistic way that impacted me and others around me. I wanted to experience God's presence in a gracious and profound way that tangibly changed my life. And, if possible, I wanted my faith to guide me and to last a lifetime. I'm guessing you want something similar.

My frustrating experience has lingered for the past twenty-five years, echoing in the stories of friends and acquaintances. So I decided to write the book I wish I'd had back then, *How to Follow Jesus*.

Throughout these pages, I hope to both spare you some pain and help you go farther faster. I'll lay out some surprising and indispensable ingredients of how to follow Jesus, building a faith foundation that will last. (All have been tried and tested by my own messy mistakes, costly missteps, and occasional spiritual successes.) I promise not to spend your time on lofty philosophies, which are better at collecting dust on the shelf than actually affecting your life. My goal isn't to fill your head with detailed Christian knowledge or even my own personal ramblings. This book is my attempt to give you what I had hoped to receive: distilled, relevant, practical, life-tested advice on how to follow Jesus.

Some of these essentials might seem familiar to you, but I intend to examine them from perhaps unfamiliar angles. You'll find other components of this foundation that you may have never considered before or may have never been able to build practically into your life. These could be some of the missing ingredients in your faith that cause you to unnecessarily struggle or to feel distant from God over time.

This book will hopefully be a trusty guide and maybe become an old friend in time. Come back to it again and again. There's no rush. You've just signed up for a lifelong marathon. My hope is to give you training tips that will help you not just endure but flourish to the finish line.

Maybe you aren't brand new to following Jesus but returning to the seed of something that was planted some time ago. You are looking to jump-start your Christian life as if it were the first time. You've been around the block of faith over the years. Maybe you've been a little on-again-off-again—definitely at church every Christmas and Easter, experiencing a powerful moment here and there, tossing up some prayers as needed—but you've always felt like something is missing. Or maybe there was a time a year ago, or ten or thirty, when you followed Jesus with everything you had, but for whatever reason your faith fizzled.

That's okay. God always welcomes his sons and daughters back home. This could be your comeback season. This is the time to restart, refresh, and renew the possibilities of experiencing new life in Christ.

Finally, I don't want to assume. Maybe you are still kicking the tires of faith, unconvinced about Jesus, yet still curious. I'm so glad to have you here. Please, don't close this book. There could be some helpful insights that will support you in making this critical decision about Christ in the coming months. At a minimum, you'll glimpse what following Jesus is really like. I won't put any pressure on you. I'll be honest about what's been tough and where I still have doubt. I'll even toss in some thoughts on what you *don't* need to do to follow Jesus because, as you are fully aware, there are a lot of broken ideas of faith out there. In case you are wondering not just how to follow Jesus but how to begin following Jesus, I've included a short segment in the appendix for you.

I've gone a quarter century following Jesus. I've walked through the highest highs and the lowest lows. I have almost given up now and then. I have occasionally let my heart grow cold. I have been stuck and I've been confused. My faith has morphed for seasons into many of the expressions I never wanted it to. And yet, I've experienced the incomparable love of Christ, the unrelenting grace of his promises, his inviting power, the strengthening presence of his Spirit, and the unmatched adventure of following Jesus which I would never trade for a single thing. This truly *is* it. Everything has changed.

No matter where your starting point, becoming new is possible and it can last. Your faith does not need to fade over time. Your best days are unquestionably ahead. Yet how you live today—how you follow Jesus right now—will always be your most critical crossroad. You don't have to put aside all your skepticism or aim toward perfection. Here's how to follow Jesus, the morning after and every morning after for the rest of your life . . .

CHAPTER 1

Your Greatest Help

Do you remember that feeling as a little kid, wandering through a shopping mall with your mom or dad or auntie? No kid ever wants to do that (unless a slushie, hot pretzel, or chocolate doughnut bribe is involved). The adults bob in and out of stores looking at shoes and luggage and clearance items and pastas. Ugh, it never ends! But then the moment happens: you knew they were here a minute ago, you were just holding their hand. You look around the rack of sweaters, nope not there; then around the side of the sock aisle, not there either. Your heart starts pounding, breath shortens, hands get sweaty. They are lost; they've disappeared in the cold, lonely, towering corridors.

They aren't lost—you are!

Not knowing what to do, you shuffle out into the main area of the mall. It is massive. You speed-walk down the halls filled with scary strangers; nobody notices. You run into your parents' other favorite store; not there either. After three frantic minutes, you stand still as people go back and forth, bumping into you with big shopping bags. Your words stumble out between snotty sobs, "I lost my mommy!" Has that ever happened to you? It's terrifying. And, yes, I know from experience. That was me when I was sixteen! Not really . . . maybe more like six; but it was still scary.

Feeling alone and isolated is dreadful. The gut-churning sensation of a lost child is the same sinking feeling the first disciples (followers of Jesus) must have been crushed by.

When Jesus was crucified and died, they assumed they had lost all they'd hoped for. They thought Jesus was going to save the day, bring down the Roman empire, and establish the kingdom of God on earth. And then he died. None of them saw that coming. "What are we going to do now?" they must have thought.

But then, as a true miracle from heaven, he resurrected from the dead and appeared to them. He ate *with* them, walked along the road *with* them, sat next to a crackling campfire *with* them. The risen Jesus was *with* them again and maybe forever; now they understood! He truly *was* and *is* the Messiah and would guide them to spiritually overcome this dark world. "Let's just stay like this forever, Jesus," they may have thought. But then, the dreadful disappearing act happened again: "He was taken up before their very eyes, and a cloud hid him from their sight" (Acts 1:9).

Jesus ascended to the Father and left them. Did these followers once more feel that churning, slicing fear of a lost child in a shopping mall? Was this the end? Jesus here, then gone again from their lives? Some of us may wrestle with this question too.

The Spirit of God

Jesus, however, left them (and us) with a promise unlike anything they'd ever known.

"But very truly I tell you, it is for your good that I am going away. Unless I go away, the Advocate will not come to you; but if I go, I will send him to you."

—John 16:7

". . . the Advocate, the Holy Spirit, whom the Father will send in my name, will teach you all things and will remind you of everything I have said to you."

—John 14:26

As followers of Christ, we have been promised something more than just a set of religious beliefs, more than just assurance of hope for eternity. We are not left alone by a distant divine being somewhere far away. We've been promised the very presence of God right here and now within our persons! We've been promised, every moment of every day, the essence of the Creator of the universe, living inside of his creation.

This is your greatest help and mine—the Holy Spirit within. We are no longer just an assembly of flesh and bones, past moments and current struggles, future hopes and crippling fears. We are now walking, living, breathing containers for the God of heaven. Wow. Sit with that.

Seriously? But How?

When I first realized, God's promise is to be *with* us and *in* us by his Spirit—my practical brain had a logic board meltdown. "Seriously? But how?" I thought.

"How do I live now that the Spirit of God is supposed to be living in me? I mean, I still need to eat breakfast, go to work and school, take out the garbage, and deal with frustrating people. Do I get to skip all of that now and hang out in the forest and wear sandals with socks while humming church songs all day long?" (I don't actually wear sandals with socks, in case you are wondering.)

"I still say cutting things to the people I love, comments that don't sound a whole lot like God. Wouldn't the Spirit of God, if he were living in me, always speak more kindly and much more profoundly than what is coming out of my mouth? I still waste some of my time and money and energy on things that aren't exactly God stuff. If God is alive in me, shouldn't he be supercharging everything I do? While we're at it, can't I get a little tap water turned into fine wine? That might be nice."

I thought of it this way, "If Spiritual Superman is supposed to be living inside of me, how do I tap into that power? How do I access God like that?"

Surprisingly, the Bible makes this very clear. Its pages are covered with descriptions and examples of what it looks like to live with the Spirit of God taking full control. In fact, it is precisely how Jesus lived, and it no longer needs to be a far-reaching mystery for you and me: "Since we live by the Spirit, let us keep in step with the Spirit" (Galatians 5:25).

That's it. The essence of God is right there inside us; all we need to learn is how to keep in step. That's also a helpful analogy which can frame how we think about our faith development: as hiking lessons for keeping in step with the Spirit of God.

Last summer I took my then nine-year-old son, Isaiah, hiking on his first fourteener (Colorado speak for peaks higher than 14,000 feet). Of course, I had to pick a somewhat difficult one because, well, I tend to make life more difficult than it needs to be. Instead of finding a hike where we could park at the trailhead, this trail required a backcountry approach the day before with all our camping gear on our backs (correction: on my back). We had an overnight in the wilderness with bears and marmots and elk and eagles; we even pulled a few trout out from the stream, and the stars put us to sleep—not a bad setup.

We woke before dawn. Pounded out a couple miles of easy terrain until we reached the base of the first challenging stretch. It was a switchback of steep loose dirt and mountain grass at a 40 percent grade for about two miles (imagine looking up at your stairs, but with no stairs). Then we hit the boulder field at least another mile long and wide. Truck-sized stones scattered carelessly on top of one another, the result of careening rockfall from countless years ago. Crevasses that go deeper than I could see. I was a tad worried about Isaiah. But this wasn't our first hike.

We'd completed many smaller peaks together. Over the years, I'd slowly taught him how to handle more difficult terrain. I'd taught him how to sidestep on switchbacks, so he gets better traction. I'd coached him to never step where your eyes hadn't been first. Stay away from slippery tree roots. Determine if your next step will land on solid or loose rock. Avoid small gravel on top of a boulder at all costs. When in doubt in steep rocky terrain, scramble your hands and legs like a mountain goat, trying to have two solid points of contact at all times. When going downhill, walk sideways in a zigzag formation. Who knew there were so many strategies to walking?

My little guy was a long way from waddling around in diapers and falling down every third step. He was now standing on the face of a 1,000-foot sheer drop-off, winds whipping all around, on a peak at more than 14,000 feet high! How did he do it? He had to learn the strategies he'd need for the big climbs slowly, one step at a time. He spent years learning to keep in step with me. We started out with little walks around the park, then the neighborhood open space, then the county paths, then the state park trail system, and finally we graduated to boulder fields and backcountry fourteeners. Clearly, I didn't start with him on a fourteener; he had to learn to keep in step.

I would tell him where to put his feet and where not to until he had a solid footing. Sometimes he'd follow my suggestions and coaching and sometimes not. When he didn't, he usually paid the price with a bloody knee or scraped hands from a tumble. But he'd get back up and begin keeping in step with me one more time (after a meltdown and a comfort food snack, of course). Now if I can just get him to start carrying all of his own camping gear!

Just Say "Yes"

This is how it works with the Spirit. Our job is to start small. Easy trails. The local park of spiritual hiking. Learn how to keep in step with the Spirit, so we can work up to the spiritual fourteeners.

How do you do this? You just say "yes." That's all. The Spirit says, "Step here, don't step there," and you just say "yes."

It might go something like: "Craig, stop thinking about what you would do if you won the lottery; it's not helping you to be content with what you already have."

My answer should be "yes" and then change the subject in my brain. But for the record, I would buy a lifetime supply of dark chocolate Milky Way candy bars if I actually won.

"Craig, when you walk past that elderly woman, look up at her, lock eyes, and smile. Make sure she realizes that she is noticed and not forgotten today."

"Craig, don't follow that clickbait hyperlink; it's not going to help you become the person you want to be today."

"Craig, pull those words back from the tip of your tongue; do not say that snarky, cutting comment."

"Craig, go and pray for that man in the wheelchair on the street. Yep, even in front of all those people walking by."

"Craig, share an encouraging word with your colleague. I want them to know that I see what they are going through and I will fill them with peace along the way."

It's not as if a booming voice jumps on the heavenly intercom system for me to hear. It's the Spirit of God within me, speaking to my spirit. It feels more like an impression or even a picture woven into my own thoughts with a calmness and assurance that is beyond myself. Over time these little "yes-es" add up and move me from paved paths to more challenging terrain.

Knowing that the Spirit of God is in you, speaking to you, is one thing. Knowing what the Spirit of God speaks is another. If the Holy Spirit is known as the "Helper," how does the Holy Spirit help? I'll unpack five ways the Spirit of God generally speaks: five pillars of support or promises the Spirit provides to help you and me. Conveniently, they all begin with the letter "P" because God only speaks in alliteration. Not! But sometimes pastors make it seem that way. These benefits are what you and I need for this lifelong, keeping-in-step-journey of following Jesus.

Promise #1—Presence

My eight-year-old daughter, Isabelle, is a craft-making guru: home-made slime, hand-crafted fidget spinners, YouTube-guided cartoon drawings, hand-spun stuffed animals. You name it, she's made it or will make it within a few weeks, I'm sure. Craft stores are her heaven on earth and pipe-cleaner and googly eyes may just be God's greatest inventions. I love this creative and courageous part of her personality.

But there is one major problem. She *hates* cleaning up when she's finished. Her mind quickly moves on to the next project, forgetting the remnants of dried glue, tiny paper clippings, and bobby pins. With all of the glitter piles and adhesive gemstones left unchecked, if she rolled on the ground she might transform into an actual fairy princess.

Obviously, we tell her, "Isabelle, if you are going to make something you need to take responsibility to clean it up too." She moans, she procrastinates, and when she's tired enough, she slips into meltdown mode. Apparently, cleaning goes against her little artistic fibers.

I used to say, "Isabelle, go upstairs and clean your room and then you can come back down and be with us when it's clean." She would passive-aggressively stomp upstairs, move a few items around, make some unintelligible noises for three minutes, and then break down sobbing.

I was concerned. "She's not responsible; she can't follow through and do hard work; she might end up failing school and robbing a bank and being thrown in jail!" I thought.

I learned a trick that helped though. One day I said, "Isabelle, it's time to clean your room, but I'm going to come and be with you while you do it. I'm not going to clean a single thing for you, but I'll be there with you the entire time."

Do you know what happened? She loved it! I sat on her floor, didn't touch a thing but was with her, talking to her, asking her questions, and encouraging her as she cleaned. And her room was sparkly clean! We could have stayed there all afternoon. She had the same passion for cleaning the mess as she did when she made the mess, as long as I was *with* her.

Clearly, I can't sit in her room every time she has to clean; she's growing at handling the messes on her own now. But just the other night she had another crafting disaster recovery operation, and my wife, son, and I sat in the hallway next to her open door and played a card game so she could be with us while she was cleaning her room. It worked and she was utterly happy.

As you walk through the messes and challenges of life which need your attention, this is the promise of the Holy Spirit; to be the presence of God in you and with you. Just like Isabelle has to clean her room, you have challenging tasks to face today, painful circumstances and tough turns ahead. God says, "I'm with you."

Like me with my daughter, God sits with us in our mess. In fact, he goes a step farther; he gets down on the floor and offers to help.

■ ■ ■

How does this work when you can't see God's presence? But just look around and you'll observe otherwise. I'm lucky to live in Denver—I get to see the sunrise on the front range every morning and, believe me, I instantly sense God's presence when I see that beauty. It may be a sunset for you. Or a warm loaf of bread, or an ancient tree, or whatever. God shows his presence through nature and the good things he puts in our lives.

God also shows his presence through people. Have you ever had a friend call at just the right moment? Or a teacher give you an affirmation you desperately needed to hear? Or a family member lock on with a warm hug? God is present through people, providing reminders of his closeness all day long.

But finally, God speaks by his Spirit to your spirit. When I am feeling cut-off or alone, I often go to a quiet place, close my eyes, take a deep breath, and begin reciting the promises of God:

. . . Never will I leave you; never will I forsake you.

—Hebrews 13:5

. . . God abides in us, and His love is perfected in us.

—1 John 4:12 NASB

Where can I go from Your Spirit? Or where can I flee from
Your presence?

—Psalm 139:7 NASB

Literal waves of warmth begin to wash over me. I hear in my
heart God saying things like:

"I'm here."
"I've got you."
"You are not alone."
"Craig, I am with you."

And then I can conquer the challenges ahead. Knowing my good
Father is with me, in the middle of the messy room I have to clean,
makes all the difference. The Spirit of God brings the presence of
God into my life and yours.

Promise #2—Peace

I've watched friends mourn their too-soon-to-be-lost teenaged children. Two young dads I know have been battling leukemia, with
death sentences from doctors hanging over their heads. I've seen
buddies lose their life savings in a market crash. Others get rejected
by a loved one or dropped by a long-term employer. I've experienced
people with stresses mounting high in their lives, but something was
different about each of these friends. In Christ, they maintained a
peace beyond comprehension beneath the chaos.

Don't get me wrong. They cry and question and cuss and grieve.
Just as we all might do when life hands us more than we can handle.
But they hold fiercely to hope, not a hope that things will turn
out exactly as they want (we've all lived long enough to know that
doesn't always happen), but to the hope that Jesus loves them and
will work all things for their good. This hope gives them peace even
in the most disheartening circumstances. This doesn't mean every

moment will be peaceful, but through continually choosing to trust and surrender to Jesus, they can experience a peace that flows like an undercurrent through their circumstances.

It's the same thread that must have been in play when Jesus was once on a boat.

He and the disciples had been working hard, you know preaching to the crowds, casting out a few demons, healing the sick, maybe resurrecting a dead guy, just your average day-to-day stuff. But they were tired, and it was time to go to the other side of the lake.

So, they jumped into a boat. The disciples grew up fishing and probably knew from the pressure changes in the air, the shifts in the wind, the color changes in the evening sky what was about to happen.

A furious squall came up, and waves broke over the boat, so that it was nearly swamped. Jesus was in the stern sleeping on a cushion. The disciples woke him and said to him, "Teacher, don't you care if we drown?"

—Mark 4:37–38

I don't think they said those words kindly with a gentle whisper either. In case you're wondering where the whole screaming "Jesus!" when something really bad happens (hammering your thumb or flunking an exam, for example), ground zero for that habit was this boat ride . . . I think. Here's my version of how it went down.

"Jesus!" they might have screamed. "We can hardly get these words out to wake you up because our mouths are full of seawater, just like this boat! Are you seriously going to keep lying there like a kitten in the sunshine? Wake up and do something helpful; like, I don't know, maybe grab a bucket and start bailing out water like the rest of us!"

Picture Jesus slowly waking up. Yawning. Extending with a slow-motion stretch and blinking eyelids a few too many times.

"What's wrong, Peter? Why are you all wet and so upset? Oh, the furious squall you say. The waves *inside* the boat. Oh, I see now."

Jesus stands up and says three simple words recorded in the book of Mark.

"Quiet. Be still" (Mark 4:39).

And instantly all was calm.

You know where I am going with this, don't you? And you are already thinking, "Yeah Craig, but that was Jesus. I mean it helps when you're in charge of the weather and have a direct line to the Father of heaven."

Please listen closely to this:

And if the Spirit of him who raised Jesus from the dead is living in you, he who raised Christ from the dead will also give life to your mortal bodies because of his Spirit who lives in you.

—Romans 8:11

The *same* Spirit who lived in Christ lives in you. The *same* Spirit of the One who calmed the waves, defeated death, and calls you his child lives—in—you.

This knowledge leads to peace. It's why Jesus could fall asleep in the midst of a storm. He knew the Spirit that lived within him and the strength of the One he could call upon through the Spirit. ". . . the mind governed by the Spirit is life and peace" (Romans 8:6).

Jesus had given over control so that peace would take over in the storm. You can too.

This isn't always easy. The Spirit is always gentle with us, and though he offers us peace, often the storm is so loud it can drown out the offer. I think it starts by doing exactly as the disciples did, turning to Jesus in the middle of the storm. Call out to him. Let him know all of your hurt, pain, and anxiety. Bring it all to Jesus and remember *who* he is. Remember *what* he is capable of. Remember *when* he called you his own. Remember *why* you don't need to worry. Remember *how* he has shown up for you time and time again in the past. Believe the promise of Scripture and ask the Holy Spirit for his gift of peace.

> The peace of God, which transcends all understanding, will guard your hearts and your minds in Christ Jesus.
>
> **—Philippians 4:7**

Promise #3—Power

Back to the boat and the squall and the mouthful of seawater. Let's not forget the fact that Jesus spoke and *stopped the storm!* There was supernatural power through the Spirit which changed the natural order. That's called a miracle, just in case you were wondering. Don't think this is just something that happened a long time ago in a far-off land; that same Spirit who empowered Christ, who raised Christ from the dead, is living in you and me right now.

So, when we pray, when we ask, when we put something before God, we should expect God to show up.

According to Scripture, God:

> . . . is able to do immeasurably more than all we ask or imagine, according to his power that is at work within us . . .
>
> **—Ephesians 3:20**

You have power, his power. When your natural meets the Holy Spirit within you, God begins to do the supernatural.

William Temple, a renowned teacher who served as a bishop in the Church of England in the early 1900s, once said, "When I pray, coincidences happen, and when I don't, they don't."

What if you prayed for the storm to stop? What if you prayed for the cancer to be healed? What if you prayed for the habit to lose its grip on your life? What if you prayed for your sister to break through the depression? Nothing might happen, because not all prayers are answered the way we understand. But what if God stepped in with power, through *you*, and brought more of heaven to earth? You might as well try to live as if you believed that truth because you have access to this power. And as you turn to him, you can be filled with this power every day of your life.

One significant way God empowers you is with gifts of the Spirit. We won't go into great detail here, but among the many gifts are leadership, helps, faith, words of knowledge, intercessory prayer, wisdom, giving, administration, craftsmanship, prophecy, discernment, healing, and evangelism.

These gifts are like a dual-operated clock radio (I'm not sure if anyone uses those anymore, but I still do!). When you operate on battery power only, the speakers aren't quite as loud and the clock won't last more than a few hours. But plug it in to a power source and everything changes: the screen lights up brightly, the music pumps out Justin Timberlake's "Can't Stop the Feeling" at full blast, and it will never die down. *I got that sunshine in my pocket. Got that good soul in my feet* . . . (Uh-oh, you're singing in your head again!)

The gifts of the Spirit are sometimes woven into our natural personalities but may function like an unplugged electronic device until we are regularly filled by the Spirit. Leadership for me is a top spiritual gift. I like to solve problems, assemble teams, achieve goals, and charge after a vision. But when I live this out in the power of the Spirit I find I have spiritual eyes to see things in a new way I never could have apart from the Holy Spirit. I can see a new strategic solution we may have been missing. I can see where I've gone wrong and need to adjust course, where I've misspoken and need to go back and make things right with a team member, where I need faith for the vision that I never could have concocted on my own. My leadership is a gift of the Holy Spirit that the Spirit empowers.

Other spiritual gifts are not rooted within our natural selves at all. They function as divine gifts that only come from the outside, from the Spirit of God. These gifts empower us to function in ways entirely foreign to our natural possibilities. Gifts such as healing or faith or even prayer are often injected into our human existence and ignite us to new capabilities for God's work to be done.

Part of your job as you follow Christ will be to discover your spiritual gifts and begin using them to serve the purposes of Christ here on earth. According to Ephesians chapter 4, the gifts are not given for our own benefit but for the benefit of others, to build up the church and to grow the things of God here on earth. So, get after it. How, you ask? By trial and error, by feedback from those who know and love you, by asking God for direction and clarity. Be bold and get moving.

Promise #4—Protection

There is a big hindrance to keeping in step with the Spirit. It's that little thing inside us called "the flesh." That's Bible-speak for the "old" you and me, and it doesn't just mean our physical flesh but all the ways of thinking and wanting and deciding that character-ized our lives before we knew God. This is the version with broken motives and little desire to live with and for God, and it creates a daily civil war inside of our souls. Knowing this explains a lot! And this civil war is not just a battle inside you and me; it's happening throughout the entire world. The kingdom of God (wherever the Spirit of God is in charge) is here and present with the coming of Jesus and his death and resurrection, but it is clashing with the kingdom of this world (wherever everything but God takes charge) until Christ returns again.

It's almost like we are young soldiers approaching the beaches of Normandy with enemy firepower blasting at us from every direc-tion. If you were one of those soldiers you would think the mission you'd been given was impossible, just as the mission to battle our "flesh" can seem equally impossible. But you need only remember one thing: *Don't worry about the enemy around you; keep in step with the Spirit. He will tell you where to go and not to go.* Thankfully, God gives us tools to help us recognize the voice of the Spirit. He doesn't leave us just guessing on our mission (we'll get into what those tools are later in the book).

So, what does this battle against the "flesh" look like in practice in our everyday lives? Remember this is an internal battle as much as an external one. We want to click on that link, say those hurtful words, watch that violent movie, fudge those numbers, sleep with that person, avoid that problem . . . and then the Spirit whispers, "Don't do that." The Spirit isn't trying to ruin our fun; he's trying to protect you and me from harm.

Here's the really good news though; the Spirit doesn't just tell us to do things or not to do things. God helps us in our time of need: " . . . But when you are tempted, he will also provide a way out so that you can endure it" (1 Corinthians 10:13).

When the pressure mounts to do something, which will clearly cause damage to you or someone else or your relationship with God, God promises to *always* provide a way out. He gives us the strength and power to live the new life he calls us to, and over time he changes our desires to match his own.

Imagine having two different plants in your garden: one is flesh, one is Spirit. Whichever plant you water, grows. Every time you choose to keep in step with the Spirit, the spiritual strength inside of you grows just a little bit more. Every time you water the flesh, saying no to the leading of the Spirit, the strength of the flesh inside of you grows. If you keep in step with the Spirit, you are good to go. If you mess up, well, just get back to watering the Spirit; the reflex will grow stronger every day.

At times, evil dangers—spiritually or even physically—will aim to take you out. You can't walk around life afraid of these threats nor do you need to. Why? Because you have the same Spirit of the one who raised Christ from the dead living inside you! Just be sensitive to the nudge of God, the whisper of the Spirit. You may have a calm, strange assurance that you are, for example, supposed to stay away from a certain person or place. Just keep in step with the Spirit and you will be protected; you need not live in fear.

Promise #5—Perseverance

As I mentioned in "The Morning After," my default when something new and good happens in my life is often to become a little afraid; I wonder, "Will it really last?" You might be similarly wondering,

"How will I live this faith out to the very end of my life?" This is precisely where the promise of God's Spirit has you and me covered. Listen to this prayer written by the apostle Paul, one of the founders of the church and the writer of much of the New Testament:

> We continually ask God to fill you with the knowledge of his will through all the wisdom and understanding that the Spirit gives, so that you may live a life worthy of the Lord and please him in every way: bearing fruit in every good work, growing in the knowledge of God, being strengthened with all power according to his glorious might so that you may have great endurance and patience . . .
>
> **—Colossians 1:9b–11**

We are called to a life of great endurance. Our faith will require more effort and fortitude and continual intention and attention. We are called to live in a "worthy way" every day and to "bear fruit in every good work." But we don't need to worry, because the Spirit gives us that endurance through God's strengthening. We will talk at length about how to access that strengthening more deeply in the upcoming chapters. But we have this promise of God: "Now it is God who makes both us and you stand firm in Christ. He anointed us . . ." (2 Corinthians 1:21).

We are not alone in this journey that will require great perseverance; we have the Holy Spirit.

This is all you really need to know about the Spirit of God: "Today, if you hear his voice, do not harden your hearts . . ." (Hebrews 3:7–8).

The Spirit of God, the same Spirit who raised Christ from the dead, is living in you, speaking to you and empowering you. You are not alone. You can be filled with his presence and peace. You have power and protection from on high to persevere until the end. Allow him to fill you and lead you and you will be emboldened to live far beyond your own capacities. This is how we keep in step with God's good Spirit. Now let's take the next step.

CHAPTER 2

Your Greatest Skill

You've seen some variation of these online lists: "The Ten Secrets of Highly-Successful, Never-Mediocre-for-a-Single-Minute People." Wake up at four a.m., accomplish fifteen challenge goals before noon, eat tree bark and ice chips, floss your back molars, compost your trash even if you live in the city, call your mom every evening, take fish oil and garlic tablets (ever smelled someone who does that?), hand make your own furniture, and never eat dessert unless it's fruit.

Ugh! Secrets-to-success lists are dizzying. Sure, they include some good principles, but often I develop a slight sense of guilt when I read them, thinking, "I could never live up to that," or "I don't even want to live up to that!"

I remember when I became a Christian some "how-to-be-successful-at-faith" lists I stumbled upon haunted me as well. Though the advice was sometimes helpful, in time, it seemed to do more harm to my heart than good. I felt I could never fully live up to these lofty goals and it drove me toward a sense of defeat. Maybe you've had a similar, internal conversation: "I want to be great at following Jesus for the rest of my life, but . . ." Fill in the blank. "I can't live it out like that polished, professional pastor. I probably won't become a tribal missionary and learn six new languages. I can never accomplish all I hear I should be doing at church; I'd be volunteering eight nights a week! I couldn't live a life like that homeschooling mom or Sunday school teaching dad or on-fire Christian college student. I'm not sure I even want to!"

To wholeheartedly follow Jesus for the rest of our lives, we must reframe what authentic faith looks like, because it *is* attainable for you even if the advice lists make you feel otherwise. Don't believe me? If you boil it all down, there is one skill you'll need above every other habit; just one secret to success. You can take a deep breath and tear up the list; you won't have to eat tree bark and ice chips and you can still have dessert. If you get this single skill right, your life with God will thrive over time. Let's look to Jesus to set the backdrop for this skill.

He was once cornered by the religious elite; they wanted to pin him down as a potential heretic and make it look like he couldn't measure up to all the rules (they had their own success lists too). "What's the most important commandment?" they asked. His answer cut through the mud of religiosity.

> Jesus replied: "'Love the Lord your God with all your heart and with all your soul and with all your mind.' This is the first and greatest commandment."
>
> **—Matthew 22:37–38**

According to Jesus, this is *the* primary point of faith: learning how to love God. And 1 John 4:19 illuminates this process: "We love because he first loved us."

So, what is our faith all about? Love and know you are loved. That's it; that's what you need to know to follow Jesus effectively. End of book. Mic drop. Sort of.

Love clarifies faith. Love even defines the purpose of our faith. Love, however, doesn't necessarily simplify faith. Wait, what? Are you throwing shade at love, Craig? It's all about love, yes, but I promised you I'd be more practical. Trying to define love and all the *how-tos* of love is like trying to describe the cosmos; where do you even begin? There are hidden elements of love, felt experiences, inner thoughts, and outward expressions.

Love in Practice

Having been married for eighteen years, I may not be able to wholly define every aspect of love, but I can tell you with confidence there is *one* skill above every other that causes love to grow. All the other stuff—like picking up my dirty socks, going out on dates together, keeping romance alive, believing the best about the other, sticking together when times get tough—is important. But every aspect of my growing love for my wife, Sarah, emerges from the single skill of good communication. If I don't grow in communication, our relationship of love doesn't work, period.

The same is true of our relationship with God. If love is the whole point, then communication is the hidden key. We cannot have or grow in love without some form of communication. The Bible has a word for communication with God: *prayer.* So here it is, the single item on my how-to-be successful-at-faith list for you and me: if we grow in prayer, we will grow in love. As we grow in love we will grow in faith and live out God's intention for our lives, to be wholly connected to him. Everything else you and I need along the way will flow out of communication with our good Father in heaven who loves us. We just need to keep the lines of communication open and active.

If we want our lives to be saturated with the favor of God, if we want contentment and joy within, if we want the peace that passes understanding, if we want the awareness of God's love at the forefront of our lives and his voice to ring in our hearts, if we want direction and strength and help and hope, then our goal must be to grow in the practice of consistent prayer. This is how faith matures into a rich, loving relationship with God rather than a dry religion.

That is so freeing!

Yet, in the same breath, it presents a very big problem. Here's my confession: prayer has been extremely difficult for me for many years. It has often been far easier for me to roll up my sleeves and accomplish something, or to do the opposite, kick back and check out when I'm tired, than to build daily prayer into my life.

Focused, distraction-free consistent conversation with the living

God remains one of the hardest things I've had to learn how to do. This isn't because God makes it difficult. It's not because I don't love God or think God doesn't love me. It's because there are so many forces pushing and pulling me in directions away from him. Let's be honest. If communication is the key, then I have some growing to do—just ask my wife.

Unfortunately, Christians (myself included) often make a handful of mistakes which cause prayer to be much more difficult than it needs to be. These old ways of thinking are pitfalls that suck the life out of prayer. We don't even realize we are making the mistakes because they occur without notice, and we end up drifting from the most important growth-producing practice of our lives.

So, let's get practical and swiftly tackle three of the most undermining mistakes we make when we try to pray. We will replace each old mistake with a new life-giving solution which will lead us to day-in-and-day-out connectedness to the living God.

Mistake #1: Neglect Your Non-Prayer Life

This sounds a bit counterintuitive, but here's what I mean. Prayer takes effort; I know it's about love and connection, but I also know communication with anyone, even a cherished spouse, can sometimes feel like work. There is no need to feel guilty about admitting prayer doesn't come easily for you. Sure, there are those occasional times when prayer is effortless and free-flowing and matches our mood; there is space for us to focus; the air temperature is just right; the coffee is still hot; and we've already gone to the bathroom. We feel the Spirit of God shining on us, and prayer just flows from our lips or thoughts. We are emotionally connected with God and wholeheartedly centered. We have some of those perfect prayer moments, but then we think every time we pray is supposed to mimic those convergence experiences. Not exactly! Prayer is soul work.

And what's required to accomplish work? Energy. We can't accomplish a single task in life without some level of energy that we devote to it.

So, one of the greatest mistakes we make when it comes to prayer is to neglect to manage our energy in our non-prayer life.

How can I prove my point? I'm assuming you've attempted to pray at least a handful of times already. What most often gets in the way when you try to pray? Maybe you try to pray at night before bed or early in the morning. Or maybe you're on a lunch break or between classes and put your head down on an armchair. Get cozy. Take a deep breath. Close your eyes. Start praying. The rhythm of your breathing takes over. Sounds disappear. Voila! You fall asleep! Prayer attempts often act like lullabies, don't they?

What happened to our early church fathers—the pillar disciples Peter, James, and John who founded our faith and wrote part of our New Testament? At the moment of Christ's greatest need just before his crucifixion, Jesus asked them to watch over him in the garden in prayer. What did they do? They fell asleep (Matthew 26:36–41)! The modern-day version might have had them drifting off into an hour of Instagram and Twitter feeds, then after that, falling asleep.

We need energy (and focus) to pray effectively. It is as simple as that. We can't just add a thriving relationship with God into our already full lives and not restructure some aspects of our time. We will need to carve out the energy and space needed to invest in prayer. Call me crazy, but this even gets down to how we handle our physical bodies in order to have enough energy for our spiritual growth.

Do we get to bed early enough to have adequate energy for the next day? Maybe we'll still get to class or to work on time if we watch one more episode of our latest binge show. But will we have enough extra energy for a vibrant prayer time with the God who loves us in the morning? If we want a rooted relationship with God, having energy available for prayer can't be an afterthought.

In the Jewish tradition from the ancient days to the present, the Sabbath (a day of devotion) always begins at sundown the evening before. Similarly, how we manage the evening before will determine if we have enough energy for our lives with God the next day.

Also, are we building times of replenishment into our lives to "re-create" our souls? Recreate, get it? Choosing to occasionally unplug and refill so we have enough energy to give to prayer is a powerful tool for faith. Don't feel guilty about the self-care you need in order to have energy for the work of spiritual growth.

I realize this is strange advice for prayer. However, when I've been sluggish in prayer at various seasons of my life, often the most helpful first step for me isn't to put together an intense prayer regimen. Surprisingly, it's to get more disciplined about my physical habits of sleeping, eating well, and exercising. As I adjust the sense of discipline over my body, it almost never fails—the spiritual practice of prayer becomes easier. I have more energy and more self-control to bring to every moment of prayer.

Remember, mistake number one is to neglect your non-prayer life. The solution is to develop an energy management discipline, so you have what you need for times of prayer.

Mistake #2: Pray Aimlessly

In my earlier years of faith—my late teens and early twenties—I had the innate passion and the natural time to pray. I would sit down to pray hoping for extended periods of deep spiritual breakthrough. Instead I generally wound up lost in thought (if not asleep), unable to think about what I would pray and probably more focused on what lunch I would choose from the university cafeteria.

Then a mentor asked me, "Craig, what do you notice about David's prayers in the Bible?" (He was referring to the psalms of King David, the man made famous by Michelangelo's statue and king of Israel circa 1010–970 BC.) I thought it might be a mind-trick question from Obi-Wan to his young Jedi.

"I don't know. Umm, they are poetic?"

"Sometimes, but did you notice? They are *written*," he said. "I'm sure there are many prayers that David muttered beneath his breath or said out loud to God throughout any given day. The apostle Paul, after all, does instruct us to 'pray without ceasing.' But if you are stuck in prayer or just new to prayer, give yourself a little more structure to get going. Why don't you begin by writing out your prayers? Literally, write your own Psalms like King David did."

I had to get over the notion that I couldn't be Mother Teresa or Saint Paul right from the start and pray every moment of the day; I needed some mental training wheels on this one. So, I put pen to paper and started writing out my prayers. This became a significant breakthrough in my relationship with God.

My frazzled mind could finally think one single thought at a time when I was writing; imagine that, a true miracle! My head felt less like a hummingbird darting from one blossom to the next and more like an eagle, focused and attentive as it swoops in on its prey (no pun intended). The more I attempted writing my prayers, the hungrier I grew for prayer. When I was finished, I had an actual written prayer on paper, which meant the little voices in my head that tried to twist and confuse me ("you didn't really pray, you just let your mind meander for a few minutes there") were finally quieted. "No, Little Voices, I prayed, and I have written proof!"

I could even go back over time and review my prayers. If the prayers were requests, I noticed the ones that God had answered as well as the ones that he hadn't. That would cause me to reflect further and pray more fervently, asking, "God what are you up to with this desire of mine?" I'd open my eyes in a new way to pay attention to his work.

I made great progress with this practice, but then I hit another major roadblock and lost my prayer steam. It's as if I'd get stuck even though I was praying; my prayers were losing their sense of power and connection.

I'd have one season where my prayers treated God like a cosmic vending machine. I listed request after request after request and then said "Amen." God does care for every little detail and hair on our heads. However, even when we pray daily, if vending-machine requests are our only form of communication with God, we have incomplete prayer lives and ultimately an empty relationship with God.

Or I would have some seasons where my prayers amounted to

a long period of navel-gazing. These were sessions of constant, self-only introspection. Most of my prayers were about what I thought, what I felt, what I needed, how I needed to change, what was working in my life and what wasn't, what my desires were, and so on.

You can clearly see the theme, right? Me, myself, and I! Again, it's important to self-reflect in prayer up to a point. But at some moment, those prayers cross over into an excuse for narcissism and mirror staring, even if they are self-critical. Imagine a relationship with a friend in which all that friend does is talk about themselves. At some point, that friendship is going to start feeling a bit fragile and it probably won't last.

I had unintentionally developed an imbalanced prayer life. I didn't even know that was a thing! Have you ever played the *Settlers of Catan*? Kind of nerdy, I know. The goal is to collect different resource combinations of grain, wool, ore, brick, and lumber in order to build up roads and cities and dominate the land. If all you have is lumber, well, you can't eat. If all you have is wool, you can't build a road. You need a balanced growth of all the resources. It's sort of like baking a cake—you need all the ingredients in some measure to get the right outcome.

Nothing we've ever accomplished in life grows properly without some patterned intention. This is true even with our prayers. Don't worry though, I'm not about to burden you with a structure you can't easily manage, and I won't suggest something that will squeeze the mystery out of our time with the Divine. This prayer structure has breathed life into my conversations with God and kept me on a holistic track of prayer, growing in love for and with God over time. Though I pray in many different ways, I still use this method after twenty years. It is based on the acronym CHAT[1] which is based around the Lord's Prayer (see Matthew 6:9–13) that Jesus once taught to his disciples.

I literally sit down with a journal or piece of paper, draw three horizontal lines creating four equal sections on the paper and write C, H, A, T, one letter at the top of each section. Here's what each letter stands for.

C = Confess

I start by bringing the truth about who I am to God. "God, this is who you are dealing with here (as if you don't know already)." It's my chance to be honest about who I've been or haven't been the last day or so and ask for forgiveness for any ways I've gone offtrack. Sometimes for me this sounds like, "God I'm sorry I was so impatient with that sales clerk at lunch yesterday. That was rude, unkind, and I think I acted pretty entitled in that moment. Please forgive me and know that I'm committed to going back and apologizing to that person."

This gives us the chance to have a candid and clean slate in our dialogue with God from the very beginning. It's us saying, "I'm going to have a no-pretense time with you God."

H = Honor

This is often the most refreshing time of prayer for me. I turn my eyes away from myself: away from my own mistakes, away from my worries, and certainly away from all the mess of this world. This is where I don't use the first-person personal pronouns "I" or "me." I only use "you," meaning God. I start by honoring him for who he is, naming his characteristics that I've recently seen or experienced or reflected on. "God, you are patient. You never turn your back. You are good. God, you answer prayer. God, you never give up on people. You never deserved death, but you took our place."

Reflect on God alone. You'll be surprised how transformative these moments of honoring God for who he is can be. At this point, your heart and mind should be sinking more deeply into a prayer focus than you may have ever experienced before.

A = Ask

This is often what we think of when we consider prayer: the practice of asking God for something. Once, before traveling, my daughter asked me, "Daddy will you bring a gift home for me?" I spent the entire trip thinking, "What is the perfect gift I can bring home for my little girl?" I chose a simple, inexpensive, colorful scarf. When I gave it to her, she lit up with excitement. Fulfilling her request became a mission and even a fulfilling purpose for me. This is how God often views our requests. God is a good Father and wants to give good gifts. He wants to know what we want and need. It's *part* of a relationship with him, not our *entire* relationship with him but a significant part.

God also wants us to ask him on behalf of others. To pray for others is one of the greatest ways we can show love to them. Sometimes, others don't have the strength or faith to ask in prayer for themselves. Or the prayer need is so big, they need an extra boost. You can stand in the gap for them. So, make sure to build moments of asking for yourself and others into your balanced practice of prayer.

T = Thank

. . . in every situation, by prayer and petition, with thanksgiving, present your requests to God.

—Philippians 4:6

Did you notice that? Right in the middle of presenting our requests, we are instructed to give thanks! There is nothing that pulls our hearts out of depression, entitlement, and even temptation quicker than gratitude. Name the things you are thankful for every day and you will find joy, centeredness, and strength like never before. End your prayer times with thankfulness and it will be difficult not to feel connected to Christ.

This time of thankfulness in prayer is also an opportunity to try out new levels of faith; thankfulness includes trusting. You and I can actually begin to thank God *in advance* for things we have been asking for, trusting that he hears us as we try on our "new clothes of faith" (concept from 1 Thessalonians 5:8) and believing that he will answer. We may thank God in advance for provision of a need or healing for a wound or sickness in our hearts or lives. When we approach God in advance with thankfulness in the present, it opens us up to see him acting on our behalf in the future.

Mistake number two is to pray aimlessly, but when instead I

start my day with intentional patterned prayer, transformation takes hold. I feel as if a crusty layer of deadness crumbles off my soul and falls to the ground. I feel refreshed. I'm filled with the peace that passes understanding. I'm undoubtedly connected to God and ready to tackle the day. When the tough times come, which they will, life-giving prayer will be our natural response because we've been building prayer muscle each and every day. Nothing compares. This level of prayer is the secret to communication which grows our love for God and awareness of his love at work in our lives.

A step for you after reading this chapter might be to commit for three days this coming week to go to bed earlier than normal (don't neglect your non-prayer life) so that when you wake up you can write out your focused CHAT with God.

Here's the final unintentional prayer mistake Christians often make.

Mistake #3: We Pray Plastic Prayers

You may have seen Ben Stiller's epic table grace moment in the movie *Meet the Parents*. His character is sitting at the table with his girlfriend's family, whom he's only just met, and they ask him to say grace. You can tell this guy has *never* prayed before. He's uncomfortable, definitely out of place among his company. But he goes for it anyway.

"Oh, dear Lord, thank you for the smorgasbord you have aptly lain before us. Day by day by day three things we pray: oh Lord to love thee more dearly, to see thee more clearly, and to follow thee more nearly, day by day by day. Amen."

I don't know what it is with our Christian minds, but I have often found myself putting up a similar veil of heart-disconnected religiosity in my prayers. Maybe you do too.

We default to praying what we *think* God wants to hear or what we think the pastor might want us to say. Or we pray what we've heard other, more "super spiritual" Christians pray. The problem is we often aren't bringing our true selves to God in prayer. Instead, we bring a pre-packaged and polished version to him. Our prayers become plastic replicas.

And what is the result? Our true selves are not transformed by his presence. Instead of showing our hearts to God, we put on a mask and wonder why we feel distant from him.

Let's consider again King David's prayers. Here's a guy with so much to lose if God or other people around him knew the full truth about what was in his heart. While writing some of these prayers, he had an entire kingdom, riches, and a reputation to uphold. Look at one of the courageously honest prayers he prayed.

> How long, LORD? Will you forget me forever?
>   How long will you hide your face from me?
> How long must I wrestle with my thoughts
>   and day after day have sorrow in my heart?
>   How long will my enemy triumph over me?
> Look on me and answer, LORD my God.
>   Give light to my eyes, or I will sleep in death . . .
>
> **—Psalm 13:1–3**

This is no plastic, polished prayer! This is a guy who gets real with his God and honest about his own heart.

Sometimes we are afraid to bring our anger, doubt, sin, or exasperation to God because we think God only wants our good. But that's the mistake that causes us to miss the power of prayer. God wants all of us, not just the put-together parts. In fact, if you and I only bring God the portion of ourselves we think is acceptable, then we are withholding the parts of our hearts which most need him.

Imagine how difficult it will be to stay passionately motivated in a practice of prayer when all we are doing is propping up a shallow exchange. Who wants to put any energy into that? Not me!

We must be courageous with our prayers. We must be vulnerable, honest, and open with what is real and true about who we are. Be willing to share the mess with God.

Notice the conclusion of King David's courageous prayer in Psalm 13. He has it out with his God and then ends up here:

> But I trust in your unfailing love;
>> my heart rejoices in your salvation.
> I will sing the LORD's praise,
>> for he has been good to me.
>
> **—Psalm 13:5–6**

Even if our hearts or our behavior are in the wrong place, if we pray courageous and honest prayers, we will begin the journey back to God. We bring what is in the darkness of our lives to the light of a good and loving God. Our behavior and our lives follow the words we utter in prayer. God's presence transforms us as we pray courageous prayers.

Just as I did with the other two mistakes, I want to give you some practical advice for getting honest and courageous in your prayers. But it's harder to give a prescription for fixing this sort of prayer, because being open and honest in prayer is largely just about making a choice, to show up with your whole heart.

That being said, a friend of mine recently shared that she finds it easier to tap into her emotions and honestly express them to God when she incorporates something physical into her prayer time. Go for a run and tap into your fear and anxiety, giving it all over to Jesus. Go somewhere deserted and throw rocks (or dishes, or watermelon) at a wall and tap into your anger, again giving it all to Jesus through prayer. Find some fabric and rip it with your bare hands as you pray about something you are grieving, something that feels beyond mending. Getting physical with our prayers can help us to feel and express the emotions we sometimes keep hidden below the surface.

What courageous prayer is it time for you to start praying? What is a step of new intention toward prayer that God is inviting you to take?

The Secret to Success

I hope that this topic of prayer didn't feel overwhelming or discouraging, like one of those secret-to-success lists we talked about at the beginning of the chapter. The truth is, prayer can be hard at times. There are a lot of reasons to avoid prayer: grief, anger, distraction, distrust, inexperience, boredom, busyness, or just plain lack of trying.

Let's never forget, at its core, our faith is a love relationship which grows in communication and shrinks when we hold back. The biggest piece of advice I can give you is keep showing up. Keep trying. If you allow anything to pull you away from communication with the God who loves you, you are letting that thing define and dismantle you. Make prayer your priority, even when it's hard. Devote energy and time and courage into an intentional pattern of daily prayer. "Come close to God, and God will come close to you . . ." (James 4:8 NLT).

Keep showing up and communicating with the God who loves you. Bring your real, courageous self. Confess, honor him, ask him for what you need and want, and thank him. He is going to show up and pour into you. That's a promise!

CHAPTER 3

Your Greatest Tool

I sometimes think, "The problem that holds me back isn't my belief in God's ability to hear me. I believe he can and always does. The problem is, I don't believe in my ability to hear him."

When you are starting to pray, and you are hoping to hear from God, have you ever, like me, irreverently wondered: "Am I having a desert-island chitchat with myself? Or, am I really talking to the Creator of the universe right now?"

The truth is, communication with anybody doesn't come that easily or naturally to me. Maybe not to you, either. If I'm not that great at communicating with people who are sitting right in front of me, how about communication with the Divine, unseen Maker of heaven and earth? It can seem confusing—at least to me. What does it mean to hear his voice, to know his ways, and to understand his heart? I need help finding my way. Thankfully, God realizes this about me and about each of us.

God knows that we didn't come to faith in Christ expecting to be stuck in our own heads, alone with our thoughts, wandering around confused and distracted. He knows we need guidance and clarity from him. He's aware of how often we are desperate for reminders of truth, words of grace, whispers that heal, battle cries for the day, and direction for a lifetime.

So, God created a solution: the greatest tool to receive what we need from him—his Word. The Bible is a written account of his interactions with humanity across time. Though God speaks through his Spirit, as we've discussed, the primary filter through which we hear and confirm his voice today is his Word. When we hear his voice, it will *always* line up directly with Scripture because God never contradicts himself.

Listen to some of the Bible's own self-descriptions. As you slowly read each one, ask, "Where could I use some of this in my life?"

A lamp	Snow	Sword	Milk[1]
Light	Fire	God's breath	
Medicine	Hammer	Plant of life	
Rain	Food	A seed	

The Bible is the most powerful tool we have to grow into the people God created us to be. Period. If we struggle in our own ability at hearing God's voice, the answer is to become more deeply rooted in God's Word, and his voice will become clearer. Listen to these clarifying statements:

Your word is a lamp for my feet, a light on my path.

—Psalm 119:105

The unfolding of your words gives light; it gives understanding . . .

—Psalm 119:130

For the word of God is alive and active. Sharper than any double-edged sword . . .

—Hebrews 4:12

All Scripture is God-breathed and is useful for teaching, rebuking, correcting and training in righteousness, so that the servant of God may be thoroughly equipped for every good work.

—2 Timothy 3:16–17

If you want to grow, you must be rooted in God's Word. But that's not as easy as it seems.

At first, admittedly, the Bible is difficult to read. There, I said it! Some people insist the Bible is simple to understand right away, and I insist they aren't really reading it then. Saying the Bible seems overwhelming is a massive understatement.

I remember picking up the Bible for the first time as a new Christian thinking to myself, "This thing is daunting! It's like the spirituality phone book (anyone remember what a phone book was?). Most print Bibles weigh a good eleven pounds (yes, of course there are Bible apps—more on those later), are written on tissue paper to fit more pages, include words I've never heard before, customs from another time, and names from an ancient world.

"Where do I even start? In the Old Testament and go page by page, or in the shiny New Testament? Do I just say a prayer, flip open the pages like Bible roulette, and jump in anywhere? How am I supposed to read this book and somehow hear the voice of God for my life right here and right now?"

Maybe you can relate to some of this. How do you read the Bible so you don't feel lost, overwhelmed, inadequate, and never want to pick it up again? Or how do you read the Bible so it doesn't seem wholly stale, ensuring instead that God's voice is clear to you each time you are reading the text? Or even, how do you read the Bible and not become a bigot, using God's Word against people? Or a fanatic, throwing down Scripture in every sentence? Or, begin speaking in old English? In spite of all these questions, the fact remains that the Bible is still the most powerful tool we have to grow into the persons God wants us to be and we must learn to read it.

Remember, our goal in faith is love; to grow in love for God and to grow in the experience of his love for us and others. Reading the Bible builds this loving communication: you get to know God more, hear his heart, understand his character, and begin to see yourself and others through the lens of his eyes and his thoughts. If you only listen to the occasional sermon at church rather than reading the Bible for yourself, it's like trying to get to know your spouse by only listening to what some other acquaintances say about him or her. That is quite limited and will never lead to maturity in love.

For the remainder of the chapter I'll share a surprisingly accessible "4Step" process for reading the Bible in a way that will help you keep in step with the Spirit for the rest of your life. Implement these four steps and you are on your way to biblical literacy, hearing the voice of God, and fulfilling life transformation.

Here is the "4Step" process in four simple words: **Text, Context, Principle, Personal**. Now say that four times as fast as you can. Text, Context, Principle, Personal . . .

Step 1: Read the TEXT

To get started, we actually have to read the text of the Bible and stick to reading it for the course of our entire lives. Surprising concept, eh? But, for it to be fresh and spiritually inspiring every time we come back to it decade after decade, we need some insight about *how* to read it.

Think of jumping into the Bible for the first time or returning to reading the Bible after a long hiatus as if you are trying get back into the gym after a pig-out holiday season. I'm well acquainted with those: tables of food every night, a schedule full of parties, and not a lot of exercise time.

You aren't going to jump on a treadmill and start running seven-minute miles if it has been awhile. The only way to start and succeed beyond the beginning is to set up some initial easy wins, not a massive plan. If I'm rusty, maybe I'll just go for fifteen to twenty minutes on the StairMaster a few times a week until my heart and my muscles start catching up again. Then I can build the stamina and actually have more exponential energy and desire to press further.

The same is true with reading Scripture for me. Unfortunately, there have been some seasons throughout my life when I've let regular Bible reading slip. I've felt distant from God during those times, eager to reconnect with him. Still, I eased back into my reading. It's important not to come back to it and say, "I am going to read for two and a half hours a day, start at page one in the book of Genesis, and trudge through all the laws of Leviticus, the apocalyptic allegories and imagery of the book of Revelation, and not miss a single day from here until I die. Go." That's not going to happen.

There is undoubtedly richness in every text, and yes, you do want to build daily Scripture reading into your life. But a picture of perfection will only kill your progress. Don't jump into trying to bench-press double your body weight with the Bible. For almost everyone, I suggest starting or turning back to the biographies of Jesus. These are the first four books of the New Testament known as the Gospels: Matthew, Mark, Luke, and John.

I'd recommend beginning with the Gospel of John. This is the most detailed account of Jesus' personal teaching and prayers. It captures Jesus himself explaining his purpose in the world and in people's lives. It's also the first book of the Bible I read when I became a Christian because that friend who invited me to church suggested it to me. Now it fills my heart every time I return to it. And so, I suggest it to you as well.

It's vital to pick a section of Scripture to read over a couple of weeks and not just randomly open the Bible each day you sit down with it. Why? Think about the gym again. If you show up to the gym and wander around a few machines, give this one a little attempt, and that one a bit of a try, it won't take long before you are extremely frustrated and seeing few results. You just can't walk into a gym and keep yourself motivated without setting a goal and going after it.

Once you've picked the passage you'll read, now you need to design your plan.

Try to think of one noteworthy or worthwhile accomplishment in your life that you have achieved *without* establishing a plan. Probably very few. Want to earn a degree, learn a new skill, run a half marathon? Then you need a plan.

Now, again, I'm not suggesting an overcommitted massive plan going from couch potato to Bible ultramarathoner in three weeks. The first part of the plan is a manageable commitment of time.

I've spent many years with the ups and downs of Bible reading plans, and I think a good starting point to let a text sink in is probably about fifteen minutes a day. Sometimes you'll spend more time, sometimes you'll have to cut it short, but I think fifteen minutes is a very manageable commitment that can get you through even the busiest seasons of life.

Assuming you haven't been reading the Bible at all, what if you set aside three days this coming week for fifteen minutes of Bible reading? Then the following week you set aside four days? And the week after that five days? Yep, thanks for asking, I *do* have a suggested reading plan for the book of John that you can follow for your first plan. Since it's only twenty-one short chapters, read a chapter a day and voila! There's your first three-week reading plan (or make it four or five weeks if you want). And if you follow the CHAT prayer method from the last chapter *and* this Bible reading process, that all adds up to about thirty life-changing minutes a day, just in case you were wondering.

Go ahead and set that goal of the book of John, then follow up with the next book in sequence, Acts, then Romans, and so on. Who knows, if you stick with it, you could read through the entire New Testament!

I've been setting and completing personal Bible reading plans for decades and it does transform me with every cycle. Sometimes I'll set just a book study or a section of books or letters in the Bible or take a deep dive in Psalms or Proverbs. Lately, I've graduated to going through the entire Bible in one year. Just fifteen to thirty minutes of reading and some additional reflection a day!

My personal secret to doing this ever since smartphones launched apps has been the BibleGateway or YouVersion or Nicky Gumbel's Bible in One Year App on my phone. I pick a reading plan that they've designed, I follow it, and I get the daily joy of putting a check mark next to each day's reading and seeing a calendar track my progress. It helps keep me going.

Maybe for you, start small and build a habit that is easily trackable with something like the YouVersion App as a tool. If you don't like reading on a device—I prefer not to—just use the plan-tracking feature on your device, and then pick up the good, old paper version so you can underline and write notes in the margin. My friend John listens to the Bible as an audiobook while driving. My old neighbor Jeff reads on his train commute. But, really, whatever works for you is fine.

Just build a plan that starts with about fifteen minutes a day three or more days a week with a pre-mapped schedule of reading. You can do it! And you will see the difference in your heart and life after just one week. And don't stop there; keep growing the practice over time.

Land your passage, map out a plan, and begin reading through the text to let it shape you.

Step 2: Understand the CONTEXT

Now, that we've cracked open the text, how do we read the Bible so we don't get confused or even misinterpret and misuse Scripture? The answer is to understand the context.

The Bible was written over the course of 1,500 years by dozens of different authors: statesmen, farmers, shepherds, peasants, musicians, poets, kings, and even tax collectors. Imagine the diversity of background and worldview over that span of time and life background.

The Bible was written from thirteen different countries on three different continents: Asia, Africa, and Europe, placed within many different cultural and sociopolitical environments. It was originally written in three different languages: Hebrew, Greek, and Aramaic.

It contains sixty-six books and many different literary forms (very important)—every type of communication is used: narrative history, genealogies, chronicles, laws, poetry, proverbs, prophetic oracles, riddles, drama, biographical sketches, parables, letters, sermons, apocalyptic literature.

And consider this—the Bible itself is one of the great evidences of God. Despite the diversity of its creation, it has incredible accuracy and consistency when it comes to the overall message about the character and nature of God and his redemptive plan for humankind. It has a single consistent plotline that carries through, unifying the whole. When I look at how difficult it is for the US Congress to come together to write a single unifying article of legislation, it is nothing short of a miracle that various authors over fifteen hundred years and diverse cultures can carry a unifying thread of God's grace and redemption in the person of Jesus. The unified text itself is an act of, and proof of, God.

But here's the problem, we don't naturally understand how to treat texts from every one of these genres and understand their cultural and historical backgrounds. Our reading requires interpretation.

You might be getting nervous now and saying things like, "I didn't really love school. I sat in the back of class and, Craig, you are starting to sound academic. Are you about to tell me that Bible reading is for professionals only? Is this just for seminary professors, pastors, and the Pope?"

Not at all! The truth is that we are already interpreting the Bible whenever we read it. So the key isn't to become an *interpreter*, but to become a *good* interpreter. Interpretation can be done by anyone, I promise (even though some seminary professors are getting a little nervous right now). We must understand that the text is layered with levels of meaning. The deeper we go into our research, the more we can find and understand. The task of interpreting the Bible is never done, as there is always an abundance of richness for us to find there. But for our purposes, as we are getting started as interpreters, we are talking about everyday-life, accessible-to-anybody Bible interpretation.

We are constantly interpreting everything we read: the news, a novel, a history book, the Bible, anything. A current event happens, and one news station says it one way and another says it another. Then one listener hears it one way and another hears it differently. That's all interpretation. We bring to the text all that we are— all our experiences, culture, doubts, fears, perceived definitions of words and concepts—and that's why we get tangled up.

Sometimes we can read into the text something that might never have been intended. Or alternatively, we can miss something that is explicit within the text because of the lens we overlay upon the context. For example: Imagine it's 3020 now and you are an archaeologist. You probably rode to work on a hoverboard and passed a levitating, gull-wing DeLorean on the way. You get to the project site and discover a fossilized headline clip from the newspaper from the year 2020. It reads:

Broncos Trample Patriots!

On the surface you (and other like-minded people) might assume there was a great natural disaster in 2020 when wild horses rampaged the land and killed many nation-loving folks. You would be so certain about your perspective that you would hold professorships, write popular bestselling books, and stir up fear and commotion among horse lovers everywhere.

Instead, if you were able to do a little more historical research you might gain some good intel on the context behind that headline. "Oh, they used to play this game in which man-boys in tight pants would chase other man-boys in tight pants, and wrestle each other, and grunt and bump helmet heads, and toss around some kind of a leather ball. And it seems the team from Denver, the Broncos, must have beaten the team called the Patriots." (I live in Denver, by the way.)

I know that's simplistic, but hopefully you get the idea. We can read into the text what we think we know and, unfortunately, what we don't know. We interpret every single byte of information that comes to us.

To get to the God-breathed, life-transforming meaning of the Bible, we must avoid faulty interpretation. Bad interpretation has been used to justify terrible things such as slavery and the Spanish inquisition. It also undermines our trust in Scripture and lessens the power and potential we can experience in our study of Scripture. The antidote to faulty interpretation is not to try to read the Bible with *no* interpretation, which, as we've already discussed, is impossible.

The answer is to learn how to read it with contextualized, good interpretation. Before we can figure out what God is saying to us here and now, we must understand what God was saying to the people he spoke to back then and there. We have to learn a bit about the original historical context and the meaning of the original written content. While there are layers to meaning, especially when reading prophetic passages, a text cannot mean something that is entirely divorced from the context of the Bible.

It's important to understand that every verse is placed not only within the context of the chapter and verses around it but also the context of the book in which it's written, the context of the section of the Bible where it appears (for example the books of law, the prophets, the letters written to the church), and also the context of the entire Bible as a whole.

To understand the context, I like to ask four familiar questions of everything I read: Who? What? When? Why?

Who? Who wrote or spoke this? What was going on in the person's life before, during, and afterward?

What? What literary form is the author using, because it determines our interpretation. Imagine trying to read Shakespeare's *Romeo and Juliet* as if it were a play-by-play instruction manual on wise decision-making. It won't help you there!

Here are some examples of biblical literary forms:

Poem—uses metaphorical language and images intended to stir emotion
Letter—straightforward communication for a particular recipient or group of recipients
Chronicles—historical account
Jewish Apocalyptic literature prophecies—encoded imagery for communication during times of oppression or foreign occupation

Some of these genres are meant to be taken literally as to what actually happened. Others are heartfelt reflections. Some are prophetic images and coded language for current events of the time. And so, we must read them differently.

When? When did the author write? What time period? What was happening to shape his perspective or intention? A war, a time of peace, occupation by foreign soldiers, infighting from specific groups of people? Were there any guiding traditions and customs specific to that time and that culture?

Why? Why did the author write this text? Was he trying to communicate something to a very specific group of people, as was the apostle Paul when he wrote a letter to the church of Corinth to address a particular problem based on traditions from that time?

Or was the purpose to establish a set of laws for an entire nation of people for the next thousand years until fulfilled by the promised Messiah? The interpretations of those two comparative reasons for writing will be drastically different.

■ ■ ■

Now let's practice the "who, what, when, why" method by studying one of Jesus' teachings in context.

"And if your eye causes you to stumble, pluck it out. It is better for you to enter the kingdom of God with one eye . . ."
—Mark 9:47

Holy smokes, Jesus, that doesn't even make sense! Which reminds me: There's a story about Origen, a third century theologian, who read a text similar to this, misunderstood the context, believed his genitals were causing him to sin, and pffft! Bad interpretation wholly applied! Historians argue a bit about whether this actually happened or not, but either way I'm glad I didn't go to his church.

Who? Jesus. He spoke these words during the Sermon on the Mount.

When? A quick Google search will tell us that Jesus' ministry is typically dated as starting sometime between AD 27–29 and ending with his death sometime between AD 30–36. During that time Rome ruled over the nation of Israel and thus Jesus was speaking about the kingdom of God in a period of great confusion over what it looks like to live as a true follower of Messiah. Did it mean that they would overthrow occupying Rome? Would victory mean physical and political victory for the people of Israel, or did it have a different connotation?

What? In this passage it's pretty clear that Jesus was using the communication form of hyperbole and analogy for emphasis and amplification while speaking to his disciples. Sometimes it might be more complicated to determine if a passage is meant to be taken literally or not, but we can turn to how the passage has been interpreted over time in the context of community. We don't have to understand the context of Scripture in isolation (in fact, it's probably not possible for us to do so); instead, we can ask questions, seek out insight, and learn from others about what's being said in the passages we read.

Why? Gouge out the eye? No. The exaggerated point is that eyes aren't what cause us to stumble. It's the *heart*! You can't *physically* cut out your heart . . . but you can *spiritually*. Jesus was pointing out that the kingdom of God isn't primarily about an external, physical kingdom such as Rome and Israel, nor is it solely about our external behavior. God's kingdom is about internal full-heart surrender and will be displayed through spiritual loyalty, not an external political power play. That is a meaty interpretation.

Seeking to understand the original context is also why playing Bible roulette is about as helpful as basing your future on a fortune cookie. You know, "Oh God, speak to me." And then flip open your Bible to a random verse on a random page. It's like a reporter who pulls a single quote and then potentially builds a whole misrepresented story out of it.

God certainly has the power to speak through Bible roulette, or I suppose even a fortune cookie (but I wouldn't count on it). However, more often than not, it causes unintentional spiritual damage and it is really based in laziness.

With Bible roulette, you are much more likely to miss out on the main point of the text and the unifying, sweeping character, and heart of God. You will miss the thematic span and possibly the intended interpretation from the context. That will only cause you to be more frustrated and confused.

Sometimes you might run into a snag and need outside information to get at the context. This is true with anything you are trying to learn. So, you must learn from other resources: for instance, a Bible dictionary, a commentary, or a study Bible with background notes in the margins. These are all easily available; try BibleGateway .com as a start.

You don't need to be a professional, but you do need to be a willing student. It will always be worth your time and investment. As God himself knows, Christians who have mishandled Scripture have caused a lot of heartache for this world and in their own lives, so put in the effort to get all he has for you from the text by learning the context.

Step 3: Pull Out the PRINCIPLE

Once we read the text and understand the context, we're able to pull out the principle. Principles developed from the original context are what can travel across languages, literary forms, cultures, and time and ultimately apply to our lives here and now. That's what we are looking for. To find the principle, often I will ask questions like the following: What does this text reveal about God? About what God values? About people? About following Jesus? About my heart?

Back to our Mark 9 gouge-out-your-eye example. While digging into the context, we discovered this principle: Jesus was redefining the kingdom of God around the hearts of people. If we focus only on the external, we will miss the truth God is teaching us.

A few other transformative principles from Scripture reading for me have been:

- What you say flows from what you think.

- Consider more what you want *for* someone rather than *from* someone.
- What you value shows up in your calendar and your checkbook (even though few people use checkbooks any more).
- God does not just want to change our circumstances; he wants to change our souls in the process.
- Our attitude sometimes determines the outcome.
- When darkness descends, the way out is worship.
- Divine gravity means that those who seek the heights of power will be humbled and those who seek the low places of service will be lifted up.

And countless others.

I often write down the principle I discover from a text either in the margins of my Bible or in my 4Step Journal. That way when I am flipping through at another time, I can go straight to the timeless truth. These principles on their own are great social media sound bites, but that's not why we are reading the Bible. It's not until we take the principles one step further that we begin to see the unquestionable wisdom of God at work within our own lives.

Step 4: Make It PERSONAL

The point is not to get all the way through the Bible; the point is to let the Bible get all the way through us. We have to move beyond informative reading into transformative application. We must transition from asking questions of the text and let the text begin asking questions of us. We have to move from our heads, to our hearts and out into our lives. We must, with God's leading, take the principles of the text and make them personal.

It's challenging to turn the mirror toward ourselves, preferring instead to grow in knowledge of the Bible or knowledge of how other people should apply the Bible. We don't want the scalpel of Scripture to be too personal, so we leave the Bible as a set of generic platitudes about God or faith and then keep living within our own status quo. Don't let that be you, or don't let that be you *anymore*. If you want the power of God through his Word to shape your life, if you want to become the person he made you to be, you must stay pliable and personally apply the principles of the text. This takes courage.

One example of the 4Step process in my own life . . .

Often, I've noticed my language is the slowest part of my life to catch up with my Christian growth. I used to try to change my language on my own: *stop saying that word or start saying those words or stop cutting that person down.* Until I started studying Scripture and learned the principle from Jesus' teaching that the mouth is only expressing what is in the heart.

This was a look-in-the-mirror breakthrough for me. I still did try to change the words coming out of my mouth, but I had a lot more heart work to do. Once I became aware of that, I could no longer add "just kidding" to a hurtful comment to someone and get away with it. I saw things with God's eyes. Clearly, I had something broken in my heart toward that person.

Nor could I pretend any longer that a string of angry words was just a simple, brash reaction; I began to recognize that those words came from anger set deep in my heart—and this needed some serious attention. I started changing the inner dialogue I was having about certain people. I spent more time with them to humanize them. I exchanged the suspicions I had toward them for benefit-of-the-doubt thoughts instead. This principle of personal application began to change my life and my relationships as the words that flowed from my life began to reflect a more positive reality of what was in my heart.

We must refuse to let the Word of God remain on the page but rather allow it to reorient our lives—every detail. It's possible! That is the power of what God has given you and me. And it is available to us every single day. Let's not just skim the surface of Scripture. Rather, read the text, understand the context, pull out the principle, and make it personal. Want to say that 4Step process aloud together one more time for good measure? "Read the *text*, understand the *context*, pull out the *principle*, and make it *personal*."

A Final Note

We cannot fully understand the text, context, and principles of the Bible, nor can we know how to make them personal, without the illumination of God throughout the process.

> The person without the Spirit does not accept the things that come from the Spirit of God but considers them foolishness, and cannot understand them because they are discerned only through the Spirit.
>
> **—1 Corinthians 2:14**

Although we spoke on prayer in an earlier chapter, reading Scripture is a process of prayer from beginning to end. We have our eyes on the text and our ears tuned to heaven, asking God for help, understanding, and guidance. When we lean into God's voice through the Spirit, the Bible will open up to us in new ways and breathe life into the words on the page.

Finally, we cannot fully understand nor apply the concepts of Scripture apart from *community*—other people in our lives with whom we study and unpack these mysteries. I'll talk in more depth about how that works later in the book. For now, we need only remember that it takes the eye-opening power of the Spirit *and* the insightful presence of others in our lives in order to reap the full impact of God's intentions for us.

If you build Scripture reading into your daily life you will be changed today, tomorrow, and for the rest of your life by the perfect power and wise care of the God who loves you. "Let the word of Christ dwell in you richly" (Colossians 3:16 ESV).

CHAPTER 4

Your Greatest Threat

T here is a Trojan horse lurking silently behind the guarded walls and gates of our faith. It is a single, massive, foundation-shaking danger which will make all other faith issues we face seem like child's play. But it's not what you might think.

If I were to ask you: What is the greatest threat to your faith, what would you say?

When I've asked others, some have quickly answered: "Sin of course." But this is rather vague, isn't it? When pressed about what they mean by sin, most people list typical temptations. Lust. Addictions. Materialism. Distractions. Obsessive-compulsive stamp collecting. (Well, probably not!)

Name your brew, whatever it is; some people fall to that risk. But what if these visible temptations aren't the greatest threat? What if they are just a symptom of something deeper? Anger, greed, and hatred are right there in front of our faces. They're like nasty potholes in the winding road waiting to tear apart our tires. But we can see potholes coming and so we can choose to swerve.

"Nope, it's the direct attack of the spirit of darkness," other people contend. What could be more devastating than firepower from the very source of evil itself? The Bible says that Satan's goal is to steal, kill, and destroy. That sounds like a definite threat, and the enemy is certainly more elusive—harder to see and understand. True, but in the most overtly persecuted areas of the world, direct attack from evil often has the opposite result of its intended effect. Explosive growth in the Christian church; emboldened faith by Jesus' followers—bravery, courage, perseverance—all in response to an overwhelming presence of evil.

So maybe the enemy is more of a parasite that you pop out of your skin like a pimple rather than an exterior threat. For the metaphor, thank C. S. Lewis; for the imagery, picture me after a personal and uncomfortable incident in Belize—no details necessary!

Finally, some might say the greatest threat to our faith is apathy. Apathy will unquestionably suffocate the last breath out of your spiritual lungs, but I don't think that's your problem. You're reading this book, after all. That's evidence you want more than lukewarm faith coasting through your one and only life, and that you're willing to do what it takes to go deeper. So, apathy is a big deal, but not *the* deal and likely not your biggest deal.

The Trojan horse threat against our faith is something the ancient writers of Scripture understood. It was woven into the fabric of the Ten Commandments. It underscored the greatest commandments of Jesus—love God and love your neighbor. However, it has been habitually and conveniently forgotten in our modern world and often overlooked by our twenty-first century churches. It's what I've personally wrestled with since day one of following Jesus. If it doesn't lead to all-out heart destruction, it maims our souls enough to feel helpless or drained when we are supposed to be overflowing with the peace, power, and presence of Christ.

So, what is it?

After the Morning After

Some of you might remember the 1990s. It was the decade of mail-order cassette tapes (and later CDs), plugged-in "landline" telephones, and all things grunge. Just picture me with a Sony Walkman, flannel shirt, and baggy, torn, stonewashed jeans rockin' out to Nirvana. This was the dramatic turning point season when I trusted in Jesus. Aside from that initial rocky start I mentioned in "The Morning After," I did round the corner and get serious about my faith. My friends will tell you, I'm pre-wired for intensity; sometimes they say this as a compliment; other times, not so much. If you ever played video games, I'm usually the guy who goes charging into the room first, then looks for what was hiding behind the corner. Needless to say, I was ferocious in my first efforts to follow Jesus.

I became "that" guy, yes, the zealous spiritual guy. The guy I didn't want to become and the person you might not want to become either. Thankfully, I was *not* the guy on the park bench with a megaphone throwing Bibles and saying, "Life without God is like an unsharpened pencil; there's just no point! Turn or burn, glory hallelujah, amen!" But I was a bit pushy with people who were close to me.

I was the guy making all my friends stay up late debating, and then asking them if they knew where they were going after they died. I was the one inviting them to church every Sunday (even if they'd said no more than twenty times) and getting into theological arguments at parties.

Please accept my apology if you had to deal with me back then.

Sure, there were a whole lot of socially awkward moments. Still, good things came from my intensity. I read everything I could get my hands on. I went to every conference I could, listened to every sermon I could find (on cassette tape of course). I read through the entire Bible, prayed, journaled, went to church a minimum of three times a week, and volunteered in just about every ministry and every capacity (I told you I was intense). I quit my job to become an intern and then later a staff member at a large, successful church (you do not need to do that to follow Jesus, by the way). I was unstoppable—or so I thought.

However, during all of my loud, busy performing for God, there was something broken beneath the surface. I started deteriorating. I was overwhelmed trying to sort out all my newfound beliefs and how to apply them. I scurried to build into my life the teachings of every book I read and preacher I listened to. I was exasperated attempting to learn a new language of faith. I certainly couldn't figure out Christians at church. But more deeply, as much as I did in the name of God, I still had an aching feeling of distance from him. I felt like I was never doing enough. And what I was doing wasn't good enough.

"God probably isn't pleased with me," I thought, and even though I was trying hard, "he certainly doesn't seem fully present with me and for me." All this performance for God never led to a sense of joy or closeness to God. The more I did, the greater emptiness I experienced. "This can't be faith! This can't be the new 'life to the full' Jesus talked about," I thought. I was wondering if I even wanted this faith after all.

Something was clearly not right. A lie crept in and told me, "If you don't earn it, you won't be accepted. And if you aren't accepted, you aren't significant." It felt like a stinging thirst on a long road trip when there was no water in sight.

Pause.

Do you see it? Do you see the lethal weapon, the greatest threat, the thing that was maiming my soul, shipwrecking the health of my heart and the foundation of my faith? I was trying to earn something that only God could give and ending up emptier and more distant than when I began. I'll tell you the theological name for this in a minute, but first the critical biblical background.

Seeking from Another Source What Only God Can Give

You know or may have heard of the ancient Israelites. Four hundred years of slavery in Egypt. Oppression, harsh labor, brutal treatment. Moses bellowing, "Let my people go!" Then the ten plagues, powerful exodus, and the parting of the Red Sea.

Well, in Exodus chapter 32, the Hebrew people (a.k.a. Israelites), now having escaped from slavery, are wandering in the hope-dehydrating desert. They are literally meandering about without a clear source of long-term food and water, and no plan for where they are headed—totally dependent on God to show up for them. They are tired, hangry, complaining. Imagine a whiny six-year-old continually asking "Are we there yet?" from the back seat (only in a caravan).

Moses, their leader, said, "You all wait here while I go up on the mountain and sort things out with the big guy. You can play horse-shoes or cornhole while you wait" (my paraphrase).

Parents, you know about the "law of the limited opportunity window," right? Whenever your child wants something, you set a precise, limited window of time to address that need or else the prehistoric pterodactyl personality of your kid comes out. Miss the window for food? Forget it! Their blood sugar bottoms out and so does all their sanity. Push the window for nap time and trade your calm afternoon plans for chaos.

Well, the same goes for the Israelites. Apparently, God wasn't following the law of the limited opportunity window. Moses was gone for forty days and the people turned to Aaron, Moses' brother-in-law, and said:

> . . . Come, make us gods who will go before us. As for this fellow Moses who brought us up out of Egypt, we don't know what has happened to him.
>
> **—Exodus 32:1**

Aaron, babysitter-in-chief for the nation, replied, "Um sure, kids, you can practice knife throwing at one another in the kitchen." That's my modern-day translation. He really said, something to the effect of "Yes, I'll make you a visible god. Now give me all your gold so I can create the statue which you will worship. Then quit your whining, will you?"

I love the next nuanced detail of Scripture here:

> He took what they handed him and made it into an idol cast in the shape of a calf, fashioning it with a tool. Then they said, "These are your gods, Israel, who brought you up out of Egypt."
>
> **—Exodus 32:4**

At that point, someone probably dropped the "bass," killed the lights, and the party started. It may have looked like street riots after a Super Bowl. Cue Moses' return.

Imagine it, Dad comes home after the knife-throwing time trials in the kitchen and surveys the damage. The text actually says that Moses smashed the tablets with the Ten Commandments on the rock in fury and disbelief at what the people had done. Then he does something baffling:

And he took the calf the people had made and burned it in the fire; then he ground it to powder, scattered it on the water and made the Israelites drink it.

—Exodus 32:20

A quick sidenote. Why do you think Moses made them drink it? I think it's because the next day when they went to relieve themselves, they would look down and see what their shiny idol had turned into, revealing its true value!

■ ■ ■

Moses asked Aaron, "Why did you do this?"

Aaron replied, "They whined for a visible god, so I just threw some shiny stuff into the fire and 'boop'—out popped this golden calf!"

Aaron "forgot" that he had "fashioned it with a tool." Can you imagine the scene? "What gold-fashioning tool in my hand behind my back? I don't know what you are talking about."

It's like the current-day Springer household: "Children, why are there empty cookie packages hiding under your bedsheets?"

Their response: "I don't know; they just *fell* there."

What's going on in this text?

The people were afraid! Worried that Moses wasn't coming back also meant God wasn't going to show up for them, either to meet their physical needs or to fulfill their hopes for the future.

It must have felt like abandonment (consciously or subconsciously). "God can't be counted on. God won't be there for us. He might not even be good or think we are good enough for him. We must create what we need ourselves, take matters into our hands, fill our own holes of heart."

They crafted an idol, a silly golden calf. This was a god they could see. A god that would not require them to trust. A god whose favor and presence they thought they didn't need to earn. A god whom they figured they could understand and control. A god-image who might work for them on their terms.

They were turning to something created to get what only the Creator can give.

Sound familiar? I do that. You might do that too.

I told you my story. I allowed my identity to be built on achievement. I thought I'd get the significance I needed in life through visible accomplishment for Jesus. Like a slowly eroding shoreline, the basis of who I was disintegrated into what I could do. I thought I needed to earn my good standing with God and build my own sense of self.

You might be able to relate to an accomplishment-rooted identity like me. But maybe not—for you, it could be people pleasing. Needing the affirmation of others, craving the onlooking eyes of an audience, unable to emerge out from under the opinion of an important person in your life.

Or maybe you have the need to be especially creative and unique or smarter than others around you, to feel that you stand out. Or maybe you are desperate for a structured, safe-and-secure, mapped-out life, where every circumstance is controllable and predictable.

There is nothing wrong with any of these desires, but instead of remaining desires, they can often slither toward becoming the obsessive bedrock of our striving souls. At that point, we have drifted away from an identity which rests in Christ and Christ alone. That's when the Trojan horse takes over; we've turned to something created to get what only the Creator can give.

Am I overexaggerating to say this is the greatest threat to my following Jesus for the rest of my life? No matter how much I may want to distance myself from this truth, I don't think I can. Nothing will take us offtrack faster than placing our trust and allegiance in something or someone (or some idea, etc.) other than Christ himself. This is the root cause underneath so many other sins that grow more visibly on the surface of our lives.

When you and I said "yes" to Jesus, we said "yes" to grace. To undeserved love. To an identity rooted in the always, only, ever accepting love of God. You said "yes" to trusting his provision and his providence with no strings attached. You did. I did. We did.

We must never forget the following verse:

For it is by grace you have been saved, through faith—and this is not from yourselves, it is the gift of God.

—Ephesians 2:8

Stop to read that verse two or three more times. Then, maybe two or three more times after that.

This love is a gift, and nothing can ever change that. If the soil of your soul should ever become poisoned over time, chances are this will be the toxic killer: an uprooted identity which says, "You have to earn God's love. You need to achieve acceptance in him through some effort of your own."

An Uncommon Word for a Common Threat

The biblical word for this identity-attacking Trojan horse is idolatry. And idolatry is exactly what I've been talking about: turning to something created to get what only the Creator can give.

Only God can give you acceptance. Only God can give you significance. Only God can give you fulfillment and purpose and security and safety and a stable future. Only God can fix what is broken and only God can give you the adventure and influence you crave. All of that is a gift from God and God alone.

Nothing in this world can provide the intangible lifeblood we need to stay spiritually vibrant and vitally alive in Christ. In fact, when we think we can get from something (or someone) else what only God can give, we place something (or someone) else on God's throne. We place a higher importance on something created rather than the Creator. We forget who God is and his rightful place, and we forget who we are and our rightful place.

Doing this will leave us stone-cold empty. Always. Trust me, I've tried.

That's why we truly have to get this one right. The root system of your soul depends on the bedrock beneath the surface. For the rest of your faith journey you will be pushed and pulled and tempted and tried. Darkness wants to win, and darkness isn't dumb. It's going to attack your identity in Christ—the bedrock; it's going to want you to put something else on God's throne, every—single—day. You are now at war.

So, what do we do? How can we ensure a solid foundation that will withstand the onslaught? Here are three practical components of a strategy to stand guard and defeat this attack.

Step 1: Recognize the Reality

This spiritual battle regarding your identity in Christ is one that lasts a lifetime. This was an overwhelming surprise for me. When I began following Christ I thought I had arrived. I'd been zapped by the Spirit through my prayer for salvation and the struggle was finished. However, once I realized I had to fight the battle for my identity every single day, it changed my faith.

You can't pretend otherwise; your faith will flourish only as you learn to let your heart turn daily to God alone and away from the idols of this world. That's why the first two of the Ten Commandments (see Exodus 20:1–6) stand against idolatry and the greatest commandment of Jesus (Matthew 22:36–40) is a pullback to center away from idolatry.

By the way, I'm not trying to scare you off here. You can do this; remember, you are filled with the Spirit of God himself and are not alone. The first step, though, is awareness.

Step 2: Reveal the Root

Think about what grows in the darkness: mold, bacteria, fungus. Healthy organic matter—good things—always need the light in order to grow (except for mushrooms and truffles—the only good things which grow in the dark). Just by seeing and naming any moment when your heart drifts toward something only God can give cuts off its power in your heart. By naming it aloud you bring it into the light, so to speak.

Here's how this works for me. I'm trying to accomplish something at work. I'm bumping into time pressures and limited results; I start getting nervous that I won't hit certain goals. On top of that some specific people in my life won't be satisfied with that performance. The voices in my head take over, "Craig, you aren't measuring up; Craig, you aren't enough here; you're going to be a failure . . ."

Then I notice the anxiety and internal pressure causes me to be sharp to others. I start using people who work for me to accomplish my agenda. I can't relax when the workday is done. I'm less loving to my wife and kids. My heart is anything but full of peace. My sense of God's presence withers.

When I take a moment to reflect, I can see that something has gotten into the bedrock of my soul. I admit, "I'm doing it again. I'm trying to achieve significance. I've replaced God as my significance giver with myself and my job accomplishments, and it's starting to break down my life." This happens in subtle ways at first. But unchecked, this is dangerous business!

Next, I bring the matter to the light and say or write in a journal, "I'm turning to performance to get the significance that only God can give" (or in past seasons of life, I'm turning to the dream of a marriage, or the idea of more money, or the shine of visible success, or the adrenaline of escapist adventure, or whatever). And then I turn to God in prayer, asking him to remind me of my significance in him. And he does, and it sounds something like this:

Craig, I bought your significance, freedom, and forgiveness in the most expensive possible way, with the life of my only Son. I have known you from before you were born; I created you to be mine; you are worth every moment of time and every ounce of sacrifice; I will never let you go. I have filled you with my Spirit, gifted you to build my kingdom, and called you my own. You are significant because I, the Creator of the world, say so with my own blood.

And then I reset. "God, I am going to let you define me and nothing and no one else, period. I will go to you, God, to get what only you can give."

This is tough work. This is daily work. Don't be discouraged if you need to have these sorts of prayer conversations often, even multiple times a day. Don't be discouraged if you need to get some help from friends, loved ones, or Christian counselors to stand strong in your God-given identity. (I have sought and still do need all that help.)

In the end, there is truly nothing else that matters. Darkness cannot steal your identity in Christ, no matter what you face. God will not let go of you; he promises to hold on to you for eternity because of his Son Jesus. *The only real threat is you and my choosing to give away the center of our souls to a lesser god; to seek fulfillment outside of the only One who can fulfill.*

So very simply, whenever fear or frustration are running hot, ask yourself this question: "What am I turning to in order to get what only God can give?" Be honest with yourself and bring that idol to light. Pause now, breathe, close your eyes, and try to candidly answer that question.

I'll give you a moment. What are you turning to in order to get what only God can give?

■ ■ ■

Great work, but there is still one last hidden layer. Behind every idol is a worthwhile need. Think back to the Israelites wandering in the desert. They desired food and water. They needed to know that God was with them and would be there for them. They hoped for a secure future and a land they could call their own. These are all legitimate needs!

But the needs of their bodies and hearts were not the enemy. It's when they allowed fear that their needs wouldn't be met that trouble began. They took matters into their own hands and shaped the golden calf idol. As fear drove them, it drives us to question the very nature and presence of God. We wonder, "Maybe God isn't here for us after all; maybe he doesn't care; maybe he isn't able to do anything for us; maybe he lied to us. Or, maybe we have failed or fallen beyond God's reach; maybe we won't ever be good enough for him, or good enough to get what we need from him."

When I recognize my need for significance, it's not bad. God wants to fill me with significance; he wants me to see that every ounce of my life is significant. It's just that he wants to provide significance in his way, not mine. That means it doesn't always look like what I want it to look like. Only his significance will meet my need, not the fleeting dopamine flashes I get from this world.

Your need might be for companionship or purpose or to be respected, none of which are bad. But, again, don't bash the need. The problem begins when we subconsciously believe the lie (fueled by fear) that God can't or won't do anything to meet those needs, and we take matters into our own hands. That's the idolatry part.

Just like the Israelites, we begin to fashion an idol with the tool of our own ingenuity. We work to create a solution for ourselves by grabbing after a relationship or after success or accumulation or pleasing certain people. God loves proactive people. He doesn't want us to sit on our hands and do nothing. He calls us to join him in the work he is doing. However, when it comes to matters of the heart, we are not its architect. As happened to the Israelites in the ancient Sinai desert, so will be our fate—not literally but figuratively.

N. T. Wright, a brilliant modern theologian, makes a bold claim that all "sin is the outflowing of idolatry."[1] As you keep walking down the path of faith, you'll find this to be true. There is an idolatry of your heart behind each individual sin. Your sins are just the symptom; it's the idolatry that distorts and sin results. If you want to battle your individual sins, don't go at them one at a time, like plucking dandelions out of your yard. Instead, attack the root system by fighting the idolatry beneath the sin. But to defeat this soul-stealing idolatry, there's the final critical maneuver.

Step 3: Find and Fill the Need

I've taken my daughter Isabelle, to a "daddy-daughter" dance for five years straight. (She's eight at the time of writing.) It's so much fun! She gets dressed up in a cute kid dress and gets her hair and nails done. I bring flowers home for her. I put on a fancy suit. We go out to a restaurant with some daddy and daughter friends. At the dance, we take a horse-and-carriage ride, dance, and eat ice cream. She smiles the entire time, without fail. It is a little girl's dream night.

Do you know what framed photos line her dresser in her bedroom? It's not Justin Bieber! (No offense, Biebs.) It's our daddy-daughter dance picture from each consecutive year, one next to the other.

My goal isn't to set my daughter up to idolize me but to fill her up with so much love, acceptance, and available presence that she wouldn't even think of going to some teenage boy to get her needs for love or acceptance met in a broken way. (Sorry to all the teenage boys out there; I was one once, so I know.)

Likewise, our heavenly Father wants to fill us up so that we aren't inclined to dig around in the ditch looking for leftovers for our souls.

More practically put, we must exchange the human way of filling the need for a godly one. Thomas Chalmers, a Scottish pastor from the late eighteenth and early nineteenth centuries, may have expressed this best when he said, "The only way to dispossess [the heart] of an old affection, is by the expulsive power of a new one."[2]

The best way to uproot our idols is to fill the space they fill in our lives with a new affection, Christ himself. We need to bring our needs, the very real needs at the heart of our idolatry, to Jesus. We can start by saying prayers such as:

Jesus, please fill my need for significance so that I can stop running this exhausting race. I'm reminded of my worth in you no matter what I do or don't do, and nothing can ever change that.

■ ■ ■

Jesus, meet my desperate need for companionship. I know the truth that even in another wonderful Christian person I will never ultimately find what I need in you.

■ ■ ■

God, you are good. I can put down this idol-fashioning tool and let you meet my deeper need. I'm choosing right now to go to you to get what only you can give.

Here is the promise straight from Scripture: "And my God will meet all your needs according to the riches of his glory in Christ Jesus" (Philippians 4:19 ESV).

Back in the days of my stonewashed jeans and '90s flannel, I began to recognize the reality, reveal the root, and find and fill the need. What I discovered was a God who didn't want to use me but to love me; a God who cared more about who I was becoming than about what I was doing; a God who wanted me to know that he was good for me, and I could trust him no matter what. The power of the idol diminished. The grind to fill my own heart and define the details of my identity apart from him subsided. I would from now on go to God to receive what only he can give. And this Scripture became true for me: "The peace of God, which transcends all understanding, will guard your hearts and minds in Christ Jesus" (Philippians 4:7).

The same is true for you. God knows your needs. He is waiting only for you to come to him. This isn't a once-and-done, all-you-need Amazon Prime package delivered to your front door. This is the daily job of clinging to him above all else, the most important battleground for the rest of your life. So, be willing to be patient and consistent in prayer, waiting for him to meet your need in his time and his way, not yours. This is the foundation of your faith and mine.

For it is by grace you have been saved, through faith—and this is not from yourselves, it is the gift of God.

—Ephesians 2:8

Something's Still Missing, Part 1: The Lesson of the Aspen Grove

There is a breathtaking phenomenon I get to experience every autumn in Colorado: the golden leaves and cream-colored trunks of aspen stands waving on the mountainsides. They are stunning, incomparably beautiful. And they are remarkable far beyond their beauty. You see, aspen grow in unforgiving and harsh conditions—stripped mountain slopes, sparse and sandy soil, whipping wind, and high-altitude, oxygen-bare air. How do aspens survive and thrive in such environments?

The answer is illuminating. You will likely never find an aspen tree on its own. Since the rocky base of the mountains prevents roots growing deep to support a solitary tree, aspens have learned to grow root systems sideways, from which additional trees grow, all forming a single, intertwined organism. What looks like separate individual trees from above ground are actually one organism—a community of trees, together, withstanding the elements.

We're meant to be like that too. When it comes to faith, we live in a harsh, often unforgiving, world. The soil is thin, the air is choking, and circumstantial winds conspire to blow us straight off the mountain. It's an enormous step to come to or come back to Jesus (congratulations!). And it's even better to set on a course of growth by keeping in step with the Spirit. But you need to know that your faith right now may be an endangered, solitary seedling on a wild mountainside without the strengthening foundation of a network of support. You were designed for community and your faith won't thrive or potentially survive without it.

The truth is, our community life isn't meant to be divorced from our walk with the Holy Spirit, our prayer life, our Bible reading, or our struggle to look to God alone to meet our needs. But because I didn't want to overwhelm you from the start, I chose to examine these "building blocks" separately, beginning with aspects of our personal life before moving on to our communal life. Said another way, the topics we'll talk about next bleed into and influence the things we have talked about previously, and the things we discussed previously also bleed into and influence the topics we'll talk about next.

CHAPTER 5

The First Response

I have a cute little beagle named Lexie. No, she's not one of those annoying, howling beagles; she's perfect. Lexie is a happiness explosion. When I walk through the door after being gone, she runs around in circles, her doggie eyes full of excitement. Her tail wags back and forth; she can hardly catch her breath; her tiny feet can't stop dancing on the tile floor—all because I'm there with her. I keep asking my wife, Sarah, if she would consider greeting me similarly when I come home, but no such luck . . . yet.

There are the occasional days when I walk through the doorway and Lexie isn't there. No wagging tail, no dancing feet, no twinkling doggie eyes. She's sitting in the far corner, quiet, shut down, not her lighthearted self. What's going on? These are the days when she's done something wrong. Maybe she chewed my son's socks or peed on the carpet or barked at the neighbor's dog all afternoon. (Okay, maybe she isn't perfect.) When something is wrong, she knows it and she hides.

This is our human condition too. When something goes wrong, we hide. Let's flip all the way back to the beginning, the first book of the Bible, Genesis (which literally means "beginning"). The author paints a poetic picture of a garden. This was a place of perfection and beauty. No sin or wrongdoing had ever occurred.

Adam and Eve, the first man and woman, were naked. Yes, I said naked. All the teenage guys out there are now thinking, "Yes!

Take me to this garden you speak of, immediately!" Though Adam and Eve were physically naked, this was not shameful. They were relationally and emotionally connected with God and each other. No selfishness, fear, past mistakes, or even fig-leaf clothing were getting in between them. But something went wrong. They turned away from God and circumvented his wise and loving instruction. They wanted what wasn't theirs to have and took it for themselves. They introduced pride, self-centeredness, and greed into the human story, and those new experiences devolved into greater destruction in the years to come.

Following this breakdown moment, God came to Adam and Eve in the cool of the day, when he would normally be with them. But Adam and Eve were nowhere to be found. God called out, "Where are you?" knowing full well where they were. Adam responded, "I heard the sound of You in the garden, and I was afraid . . . so I hid" (Genesis 3:10 NASB).

Adam and Eve hid from God.

Then, Adam and Eve noticed they were naked, felt shame, and quickly covered themselves up.

Adam and Eve hid from one another.

This is critical for us to understand. The hardwired first response to something going wrong in any relationship is to hide. It's been this way from the beginning. We hide from God and we hide from each other. Our hiding has developed far beyond fig leaves in the garden to new-and-improved, sophisticated strategies: busyness, social media addictions, avoidance, and more.

Ultimately, hiding is the wall which devolves into destructive patterns that destroy our human hearts.

Christians have designed a catchy phrase to hide our hiding: it's "my faith is a personal thing." In fact, you may have started to think that yourself, after the first few chapters of this book. Good thing we didn't stop there, because if we had, I would have set you up for failure.

I understand where the idea of faith being merely a personal thing comes from. We think, "I don't want to impose myself on others, or I don't want others to impose themselves on me. Can't I just believe in Christ, do good things, pray in private, and I'm good to go?" Building your faith through this lens of individualism however will stunt, if not prevent, your growth.

The concept of the self-sufficient, autonomous, and independent individual whom we applaud today didn't exist until the modern era and is foreign to the Scriptures we study. (In fact, the term "individualism" wasn't even coined until 1820.[1]) This cultural shift toward valuing the individual above the communal has uprooted the values of serving a common good, finding purpose and belonging in a community, working interdependently, and growing as a collective.

Don't get me wrong, there are some benefits to this shift. It has resulted in growing economies, and many of our lives are seemingly more comfortable and convenient as a result. But when that focus leads to hiding and isolation, it can very quickly become hazardous. Numerous studies have concluded that people who live in integrated community, with healthy relationships, live longer and happier than those who live more generally in individualistic isolation or veneer-level connections.

Don't worry, I'm not trying to convince you to drop democracy for communism either. But when it comes to your faith, having an individualistic focus on the self alone will stunt your growth and leave you longing for more. The writer of Ecclesiastes understood this concept:

> Though one may be overpowered, two can defend themselves. A cord of three strands is not quickly broken.
>
> **—Ecclesiastes 4:12**

As I shared previously in "Something's Still Missing, Part 1," we can't forget that as Christians we are part of an integrated whole, the body of Christ. God not only speaks *to* people; he often speaks *through* people. If we avoid intentional and authentic community we will miss out on the voice of God, the wisdom of his guidance, and the reminders of his presence through others in our lives. We were designed for community and our faith won't survive without it. To build these essential and life-giving relationships, we must break the first response and learn to come out of hiding.

It's important to mention that hiding can be a necessary form of survival in some situations. Children who grow up in unhealthy homes or people who live in abusive relationships learn to hide, and rightly so—at least until the hurtful figures change or are gone from their lives. In a formal work environment—the same principle can apply: we need a little discernment in whether to share our unfiltered opinions with our supervisors. "No, I would not like to redo these meaningless TPS reports, thank you very much," might not work out so well.

But when it comes to developing adult friendships to bolster your faith, you must learn to break through two cultural mistakes.

The "I'm Fine" Mistake

I call the first mistake the "I'm fine" barrier, which is very common in modern society. If you're not sure what I mean by this, think of how often you might respond with an automatic "I'm fine" whenever someone asks you how you are, rather than giving an honest answer. This sort of hiding is like wearing a mask. We put on a face, wear a story, and project a personality we think others want to see. We keep those people at arm's length and avoid deeper intimacy altogether.

You might be like me, who cringes at the idea of hanging out with clichéd do-gooders all day long or regularly airing my dirty laundry. However, if we live behind masks when it comes to our faith, all we have to offer others are plexiglass façades. And if the friends we are trying to connect with are doing the same thing, it's just a game of charades. You can't see through the layers of stacked-up false selves. It's exhausting to hold up a mask, and you will find no encouragement, strengthening, or connection in doing so. You'll remain hidden and wonder why life is so difficult and faith is so unfulfilling.

The Oversharing Mistake

Maybe you read the previous section, and it didn't really hit home for you. You are very authentic and don't hesitate to share what's going on in your life. Maybe you've even been known to overshare, to let anyone and everyone know about anything and everything. This may not seem like a form of hiding, but something subtle can be going on here that isn't much different and can be equally destructive to healthy relationships.

Consider social media's role. We share online to keep up with others—not just the positive happenings but sometimes the negative ones too. We want to be seen so we share and overshare, but we do it still hiding behind a mask, or a screen.

Often, we hide because we are self-conscious; we worry about what others will think or how they might respond to the real us. But we can also overshare for the same reason. In our self-consciousness we take a defensive stance and declare, "I don't care what they think about me. This is just who I am. And they just have to deal with it." This attitude also keeps others at arm's length, erecting a barrier rather than allowing for the natural unfolding of friendship over time.

■ ■ ■

Although we sometimes mistake the two, sharing *truthfully* is not synonymous with sharing *vulnerably*. Vulnerability is scary, and it requires trust. We shouldn't be vulnerable with just anyone, but in order for deep friendship and community to occur, some level of leaning on one another and sharpening one another is required.

So How Do We Overcome Hiding?

When I first became a Christian, some friends told me, "Craig if you want to grow, you need to join a Christian 'small group.' You need to begin meeting with others." That felt a little like an invitation to the vintage-era *Star Trek* discussion group at the Comic-Con convention, when I never liked *Star Trek*. Please, no offense *Star Trek* or Comic-Con fans out there. I'm just sayin'.

I somehow stepped beyond the weirdness factor and jumped in. At different seasons of my life I've experienced different forms of "small groups." Some were official arrangements through a college ministry or the local church. Some groups were friends I'd met along the way who realized we could live out the words of Proverbs 27:17: "As iron sharpens iron, so one person sharpens another."

Some groups were more organic. I'd reach out to people farther along in the faith and ask them to meet together three or four times, so I could pick their brains and learn from their lives. Often, we'd read the same book and then discuss it.

But before I could build any type of community in my life, I had to overcome a few barriers.

The first, for me, was the expectation level. I thought that since we were now Christians, the invitation would go something like this: "Hi. Would you like to become my best-est friend in the whole wide world for now through eternity, you know since we're Christians and all? Can we start meeting together next Thursday?" How awkward and ineffective is that?

Yes, there really can be unique differences in friendships now that you are a Christian, but those friendships can also be just for a season. You don't need to make any lifelong commitments or even yearlong commitments. Some friendships are circumstantial—maybe you all happen to be involved in the same Christian group at school. Some friendships are seasonal—during your twenties or while you lived in Seattle. And some, but very few, are lifetime friendships.

Let go of the expectation that all Christian community must be lifetime community, though it will hopefully go deeper than you've known before. And let go of the idea that these friendships need to become best-est. Let them be what they are: normal people coming together to grow in their faith because we know we can't grow on our own. If they develop beyond that, then great. If not, don't sweat it. This is hopefully as disarming for you as it was for me.

The next barrier was pretty obvious: "I don't have time! I've got a full class load. My work schedule is jam-packed from morning till night. I travel every week. My kids take every ounce of energy I have. I don't think I have space for new friendships."

There is no softer way to say this: you just have to find a way.

When I was in college, our group would sometimes have to schedule midnight meetings with cold pizza as a bribe for others to attend, well just because.

I know a group of business-traveling technology sales guys who are gone Monday through Friday most weeks—a different city every week. Their time on the weekends is cherished and protected for their families. How in the world can they develop any sense of consistent Christian community?

Yet they found a way to make it happen. Every Friday morning, no matter what city or what time zone they're in, they dial in to a free conference line. They share about their week, discuss the Bible book they are studying, and then pray for one another. I jumped on a call with them recently and noticed that they have such rich friendships, you wouldn't know some of them have never met one another face to face!

When Sarah and I were in the "you can't take your eyes off the kids for a single minute or they will blow something up in the house" season, we still had to figure out how to build Christian community into our lives. We gathered a few other eyes-glazed-over parents, each chipped in a few dollars, and hired a shared babysitter (a.k.a. circus ringmaster) to make it happen. We did our best to create faith-building connections amidst the chaos of "Mommy! Daddy! I made a poopy!"

Another barrier: "I've tried. I couldn't find any groups. The church didn't call me back when I left a message. No one has invited me out to coffee. There's really no one else around. This community thing just isn't going to happen for me."

This is a tricky one. Often churches and college ministries will have a great system to help you with community creation. And if you are lucky enough to plug in to something already in place and streamlined for you, then great! But this is not always the case.

When Sarah and I were crazy and courageous enough and freshly armed with our master's degrees, we moved to Prague, Czech Republic, to start a church with a Czech friend of mine. I'll leave those stories for another time, but here's a window into something I deeply struggled with. My prayers went like this:

God, I felt like you brought me here, but I feel so alone. I can hardly speak the language and when I do it's like I'm not even myself. Most Czechs are highly guarded and only let a handful of people into their lives. What's more, this is one of the most atheistic nations on the planet. I can't find any Christian community. How do you expect me to grow, God? You called me here. Aren't you supposed to solve this problem for me?

The response I sensed from God was a gracious version of "time to put your big boy pants on, Craig." More specifically, it was, "Craig, you have to create the community your faith requires. If no one is inviting you into it and you can't find it, then build it."

Whoa. Where did I get this idea that the ingredients I would need for my own growth would always be delivered to me on a silver platter of premade readiness? (Maybe growing up in the entitled West? But I digress.)

You and I need community for the sake of our own faith; our souls will suffer without it. It might surprise you that not every Christian out there has read this chapter in this book—though it pains me to think it! Not everyone out there will be as aware of or as intently committed to fulfilling this need as you will be. You might need to take ownership of this one without the initial support of an effective, preexisting system or structure or someone moving toward you.

You might need to quickly become the one who finds a few friends or makes a few new friends and build the community your faith requires. It's pretty simple, really. It goes something like this:

Find some people who are committed to following Jesus and exhibit Christian qualities you admire, and say something like,

"Hey, I'm newer to the Christian faith, but I'm trying to take realistic steps to grow. I'm thinking of reading the book of Romans (or, pick one of the Gospels) and would love to have a couple of people willing to talk it out with me. Are you interested in meeting a few times for coffee and conversation about what we read?"

Boom. That was easy. You just created the community your faith requires. Well, almost. At least you started it. Notice how low-pressure and basic the expectation? As with all good things, developing community is a process; it takes time and it has to start somewhere.

Of course, I'm assuming you are hoping for more substance than just a few coffee talks with your Christian community. Let's go a few clicks further in; we'll cover one additional, significant barrier here and the final one in the next chapter. Yep, it needs an entire chapter.

Once you start meeting with others, you have a choice. You can keep the conversation informative or guide it to become transformative. You can stay at the level of "what do you think about that Bible verse or that chapter in that book?"—like answering every question with "I'm doing great" or "I'm fine," or maybe even sharing something that sounds authentic but doesn't let anyone see your heart. However, you will only experience the vapors of community potential and not the real thing. You may even think, "Hey, this Christian community stuff is not as impressive as Craig said. I want my time and the price of this book back. I can do this just fine on my own."

However, for community to work the way God intended, you have to take the mask off.

I have been meeting with the same group of guys for more than thirteen years. We call it "man-group." I know, I know, that sounds like we wear belts and suspenders at the same time. None of us even has thick beards or knows anything about auto repair or hunting—but let us at least pretend.

It started as just a simple Bible study and developed into much more. Looking back, we have been the ones in each other's lives at every important moment. We buried the father of two brothers in our group. He died suddenly, tragically, and way too young, leaving a gaping hole in the hearts of his family and community. We all piled up, went across country, and wept on each other's shoulders at his funeral. We hugged and prayed together when another one of the guys found out his son was confirmed to have Down Syndrome. Now, he is the cutest, most joy-filled boy I know. We've also walked alongside a friend whose wife left him for another man. We were the crazy dancers at each other's weddings; we were the first visitors in the hospital for each other's babies; we have been the ones, week after week, to support and challenge each other, call foul when necessary, give a boost almost always, and pray and pray and pray together.

My wife has a similar group of women she's walked with for over a decade. What started as a weekly discussion group that met over appetizers and an occasional glass of wine grew into shared life together—friendships through the ups and downs, growing in faith and supporting one another. Then they moved for various reasons to different parts of the globe. But that didn't stop their connectedness. Now they send each other Marco Polo messages (a video messaging app for groups) a few days a week. They share what's going on in their lives and ask each other the tough questions. Sarah can't imagine a week without this group in her life, though the members live thousands of miles apart!

This kind of rich community doesn't just happen overnight; it takes time and intention. It didn't start like this; we built it this way. I want to share with you the practical step my man-group took to developing this kind of community. Every week we met, we answered three masks-off questions of one another.

Question 1—How Are You Doing, Really?

The "really" is the key. It's like saying "I want to know how you are doing, and I don't want you to answer as if I'm your office coworker or a passerby on the street or some random stranger reading your social media post. I want to know what's beneath the mask."

The answers to this question are as wide-ranging as the emotions of any person, but no fake answers are allowed! Sometimes I might answer, "I'm feeling sad this week; I keep making the same mistake in my communication with Sarah, and it's putting a heaviness on our relationship that I don't want there. But I'm also excited because we are finally finishing a project at work that has taken five months of planning. I can't wait to roll it out."

After we grew more comfortable with each other in man-group, there were the occasional times a guy would fake it and give the equivalent of an "I'm fine" answer. We'd call him on it and say, "C'mon man, we really want to know *you*. Dig a little deeper and tell us."

Question 2—Where Are You at with God?

I'm sure you can improve the grammar of this question, but it's what we've been asking each other for thirteen years, so there's that. This not only creates some space for sharing; it's also helpful for self-reflection. How often every week do you ask and intentionally put to words a response to the question, "Where am I at with God" on your own? Probably, by default, not very often. It's helpful to have a group keeping you consistently on point with these practices that will shape and sharpen you.

Sometimes you might answer, "I'm doing great! I've felt connected to him; I've read the Scriptures and prayed regularly. I sense the presence of his Spirit throughout the day. I routinely reflect with gratitude about my relationship with him. I put my head on the pillow at night with a sense of fulfillment and spiritual centeredness." Or, you might respond, "I'm not even sure. It's felt like a silent and empty week for me, spiritually. I'm struggling to push back the voices in my head telling me I'm on my own. This week has been a draining fight, and I guess I feel distant from God."

Although that second response is tough, it is powerful to communicate what is real about you with other real people who care. You will find strength just in communicating that truth.

Question 3—What Are You Working On in Your Life Right Now?

We honestly don't want to come together to hear only how each guy is doing. Although that is valuable, we want to know what each is doing to change how they are doing. As uncomfortable as it is, you want people in your life asking you this question. It has the same effect as the personal trainer at the gym. You can go to the gym on your own; once you know how to do the exercises, you really don't need anyone else there. But the power of someone urging you to give your best, encouraging you when you are discouraged about your progress, and calling you out when you give up too soon is indispensable. You need this in your faith.

Your answer could be like one of mine has been: "I'm trying to grow in patience these past few weeks. I've noticed a pattern of being quick to snap or quick to speak judgmentally. I can tell the people around me haven't been having a good time because of the heaviness of my own reactions. I've got to change. I'm praying about it. I'm journaling about it. I'm biting my tongue and occasionally stepping outside before speaking. I'm asking others, including you guys, to call me out on it. I want to work on patience."

Every now and then we might go to the next level and make a commitment about how we are growing. We might plan something like "to help me grow in my patience next week, I've set up a time on the calendar where Sarah and the kids get to personally rate my level of patience with them for the week and then give me feedback. I'll also be memorizing two Bible verses about patience and reflecting on them each day. Will you guys ask me how this went next time we meet together?"

One closing thought to help you with this journey. Therapists have written volumes on the motives for our hiding. We might hide without realizing it because subconsciously we think we aren't fully acceptable. Often in a group context, we might hold back, assuming, "They won't want to be around me if they know this under-the-surface truth about me." If we are uncomfortable or down on ourselves, we might reactively think, "I'd better put on a 'fig leaf' in the form of a verbal Facebook post with a positive spin."

When I risk heart exposure with my man-group, I still feel fear and anxiety even after all this time. But as I go ahead and share my inner thoughts despite my worry of rejection, I discover the opposite. The less I pretend, the more real friendship and respect from the other guys I gain. The more open I am, the more acceptance I receive. God's presence through community becomes one of my greatest sources of belonging and transformation. You can experience the same.

■ ■ ■

The only way to break the first response of hiding is to be intentional. Do not fall into the faith-numbing illusion that following Jesus is just a personal thing. It doesn't work that way. You have to take steps toward others. Start somewhere. Let the process take time. When ready and in the context of consistency, introduce the three masks-off questions. Be the one to take the first risks: to invite, to share, to model those characteristics you yourself want to receive from others. If you build the community your faith requires, you will experience strength, fulfillment, and joy you could never find on your own.

CHAPTER 6

The Second Garden

The Bible begins and ends with gardens. The garden in the beginning is pristine Eden—it is full of unity, continuous joy, love, and truth. All that was made was declared good. Everything was growing and interacting just as God had intended: there was no sin or death, no conflict or ill motive, no fear or greed. We were created for Eden, the first garden.

The last garden is a garden-city, one of heavenly restoration and renewal. In fact, many scholars make the case that it's not just Eden restored, but Eden fulfilled, having reached all the potential God envisioned for it. Described in the final book of the Bible, Revelation, it is figuratively named the New Jerusalem, a prophetic vision of the age to come. A crystal-clear river flows through it with the Tree of Life and healing leaves planted on either side. Here the thirsty have been quenched, the hungry have been fed, and the wounded have been healed. Here the Lord makes everything new. As Revelation 21:27 declares, "Nothing impure will ever enter it." All sin and sadness and violence and pain have been purified. It is a community of peace and perfection.

But we have a problem. When we become Christians, we begin to hope again, as we should. We tap into a longing deeply set within our souls for the ideal, original Eden. We begin to crave the complete restoration of the heavenly New Jerusalem. We see glimpses of the love, acceptance, freedom, and purpose in our new Christian friends and church communities which matches this yearning within. We start to think, "Yes! This might be it! This is what I've been made for. This is the perfection I've always dreamed was possible!" But then something devastating happens: humanity shows its face and begins to crush our hopes.

In order to thrive, we must learn that, though we long for a return to Eden and the future perfection of the New Jerusalem, we do not yet live there. We must learn to live in the imperfect here and now. This is the garden of the present age—the second garden between the first and the last. It's the garden of both-and, of now and not yet. It is both the kingdom of light and the kingdom of darkness, both the kingdom of promise and the kingdom of pain, both the kingdom of God and the kingdom of this world intertwined in exquisite fury and complex mess. You and I do not live in Eden and you and I do not live in the New Jerusalem. We live on streets and avenues, in towns and cities, among the imperfect and impure.

When I first became a Christian, I started regularly attending a church and formed a small group (I hope you will do the same). However, I ideally assumed that when I walked through those church doors or showed up to the group time, I was leaving the vortex of the world's humanity and stepping into Eden or through the gates of heavenly New Jerusalem. Of course, I didn't think of it in those terms. I probably thought something like, "Well, we're all Christians here. Things will be perfect—or at least way better than out there."

Instead, what I discovered was a bunch of people full of goodness and gossip, purity and pornography addictions, kindness and greed, prayer and pretension, reliance on God and resentment toward others. What a letdown! Not only did it cause me to question the church; on my worst days it caused me to question Christ himself. I now know you can't judge Christ because of Christians, just like you can't judge an amazing ice-cream sundae because some people ruin it by adding nuts.

I had to quickly learn that joining a church community meant linking up with people who are walking through real lives with hurtful divorces, medical catastrophes, job losses, anxiety issues, self-centered streaks, passive-aggressive tendencies, destructive patterns, internal struggles, troubled families, and faulty faith. This is no Eden. To join a Christian community is to join a broken community. It is to join with people who are still growing and who are yet incomplete.

And because of that, you can be guaranteed of one thing: you will become disillusioned. Sit with that for a second. Do you still want in?

Is that a bad thing, to be disillusioned?

No. For community to work, we must let the euphoria die down and allow disillusionment[1] to set in. Disillusionment is required. Facts are our friends. The question is, what will you do when you become disillusioned? How will you react?

I know too many Christians who for five or ten or even fifty years have been wandering spiritually, living pseudo-isolated, weakened, unfulfilled lives—susceptible to the slightest storms. Their past is littered with a series of false starts and trashed attempts at Christian community because they couldn't handle the reality that Christian community is far from their ideal, neither Eden nor New Jerusalem. So, they subtly give up and try to go it alone and then pay the price with an oxygen-deficient faith.

It's only when we are appropriately disillusioned that we are finally equipped to build community the way Jesus did.

Stay at the Table

There is a moment in the Gospels, the biographies of Jesus, when Christ pulled together his small community—the disciples—around a table. Picture da Vinci's *The Last Supper* (no, not the food-fight parody version).

Jesus had been pouring himself into relationship with these twelve guys for three years. They likely barbecued around campfires, high-fived each other when they caught fish, told stories of their wild childhood memories. I can picture Peter, after knocking down a few roasted tilapia, saying, "Guys, I've got to tell you about the time when I went sheep-tipping with my buddies. The sheep just 'bah-bah-bahed' until we had to sprint through the fields to get away from the shepherds; it was epic!" Jesus replies with a solemn, blank stare. That's how it went down in my imagination, at least.

Beyond the regular ups and downs of hanging out, they saw Jesus perform miracles and even experienced a few themselves. They were immersed in Jesus' teaching and way of life. And now, Jesus brought them to this special meal.

What happened around that table? Well, they talk about betrayal. One of them, who is secretly plotting to defect and turn Jesus over to face a death sentence for a few pieces of silver, adamantly denies Jesus' insistence that he would become a deserter. After that incident, the disciples argue about who is the greatest among them, positioning themselves to get the upper hand. Obsessed with power, fear, and stubbornness, they probably went on to argue about who was going to pay the bill and who would get the donkey from the donkey valet!

This was Jesus' "church" at the time, and what a bloody mess it was (as my British friends like to call it)!

Here's the hinge: what does Jesus choose to do in the midst of the imperfect mess? Does he throw up his hands and storm out? While walking out the door, does he figuratively stomp his Messiah feet and say something like, "You guys were supposed to be better than this; you're Christians!" (Actually, the term "Christian" didn't even exist yet.) Does he stuff his feelings, slip out the back door, then just disappear from the community? Does he give up on this group and try to find a new and improved version?

No. As one author has said, Jesus *stays at the table*.[2] He breaks bread and drinks wine with his guys. He keeps building into them and walking forward with them. He understands they were no longer in Eden and not yet in the New Jerusalem. They were living in the second garden of both-and, of now and not yet. And because of Jesus' persistence and the legacy of that messy, early community, billions of lives are now swept up into the love of God, the grace of Christ, and the presence of the Spirit.

Biblical community is *broken* community. Biblical community never fully measures up, but it is also powerful, beautiful, and purposeful beyond measure. We can discover and share that power, beauty, and purpose in our lives if we stay at the table as Christ did. Yes, there are times and reasons for necessary endings and new seasons of transition, but too many of us make those decisions too quickly and too easily, with little effort at staying. In Christ's case, painful conflict, bitter pride, and even gut-wrenching betrayal were at his table, but he stayed.

We grow when we stay at the table.

How Do We Stay at the Table?

The apostle Paul also knew what it meant to stay at the table. Among the churches he founded throughout the Mediterranean region was the church in Corinth. If the city was known for its sinful ways, the church was no better: full of incestuous affairs, lawsuits, divorces, idolatry, huge egos, doctrinal infighting, sexual impurity, and even people getting drunk at communion! How did Paul respond to all this? He didn't just walk away. He stayed engaged with this church and called them to something more—the kind of transformation through the Spirit that puts to death such behavior.

It was to that incomplete community that he penned this reminder in 1 Corinthians 13: "Love is patient, love is kind . . . it is not easily angered, it keeps no record of wrongs. It always hopes, always *perseveres*" (emphasis added). These words were not originally meant for weddings; they were directed to everyday life in a church.

If we want to grow in love, for our own spiritual sake and the sake of others, then we too must patiently persevere. We must stay at the table, even when disillusionment sets in. But *how* do we do this?

Here's the backward first step to staying at the table and flourishing in the second garden.

Realize you have bad breath too.

There's nothing worse than being around a close talker and inhaling the fumes of his triple-garlic, horseradish, chipotle pesto aioli avocado toast. Every few words seem to begin with the deadly letter "h." "Hi, how are you doing? How's the weather? Have you been to that new restaurant on Hampshire Avenue? Holy smokes, the halibut is heavenly." There aren't enough mints in your pocket that you can kindly offer him to calm that smelly storm.

The problem is, I've been that guy and I've never known it; maybe you have been too. We can't really smell our own bad breath and we rarely realize the effect we have on others, spreading our own dragon air. This is true of our broken behavioral impact on Christian community as well.

Jesus puts it like this.

> "Why do you look at the speck of sawdust in your brother's eye and pay no attention to the plank in your own eye? How can you say to your brother, 'Let me take the speck out of your eye,' when all the time there is a plank in your own eye? You hypocrite, first take the plank out of your own eye, and then you will see clearly to remove the speck from your brother's eye."
>
> **—Matthew 7:3–5**

Yeah, that feels a little abrasive, but those are Jesus' words, not mine. Jesus was speaking to a group of religious folks who were trying to clean up everyone else instead of themselves. Modern translation: "Realize you have bad breath and focus on your own Listerine moment first; then you can kindly help others in small ways with their issues."

When we redirect our evaluation energy toward ourselves, a few tectonic shifts occur.

First, we see the reality that we are part of the problem within this Christian community. Some of the problems exist because we brought them into the church. Sometimes what we don't like in others is really their reaction to what they see in us. For example, when people act defensive, it can often be a result of something offensive we've said or done. We look at their defensiveness with disdain, but we may have played a part in stirring it up.

Second, we begin to learn this mantra that took me many years to acknowledge: *if you spot it you got it*. Often when our frustrations toward others are triggered, it's because we see a trait in them we admittedly despise in ourselves. Have you ever had conversations in your own head like the ones I've had? "I really don't like being around John. It only took me one conversation with him to see how judgmental and dismissive of others he is. He jumps to quick conclusions about them and doesn't even try to understand what's going on in their lives. Yuck. I'm going to stay away from him!"

Did you see it? I created the same negative spin about John in my head for which I was judging him. I spotted what I didn't like in him because underneath the surface I do the same thing and don't like it about myself. We need this kind of self-awareness with others, so we can develop the humility required for community.

Third, when you realize the only Christian you can control is yourself, you'll begin to see a powerful pattern emerge. The more Christlike your own humble "my plank first" self-examination, the more people will want to be with you and be influenced by you. Your "plank-work" will inspire and assist them in removing what's broken in their lives. This builds the health of your Christian community through a holistic cycle of everyone focusing on their own growth and then everyone growing together.

This only happens, however, if you don't bail. You need to be willing to stay at the table, not condemning but working together toward transformation in love.

Finally, once you have looked at yourself in the mirror first, now you are able to put on Jesus' glasses when looking at others. Remember in the first section of this book the verse I suggested you never ever forget? You have it memorized for the rest of your life, right? I'll help you out again just in case:

For it is by grace you have been saved, through faith—and this is not from yourselves, it is the gift of God . . .

—Ephesians 2:8

Now read that verse and insert the name of a person at church who frustrates you.

For it is by grace that _____ has been saved, through faith . . . it is the gift of God.

In Christ, he or she, no matter the behavior, has received exactly what we have received: grace from God. Sometimes I can receive this grace for myself, but when triggered by others' humanity, I have difficulty applying the same grace to them. Here's a summary account from the life of Christ that both challenges me and teaches me toward this end:

A wealthy man once ran up to Jesus. He was successful, but materialism had clearly crept into his soul. His priorities were off. He was hoarding for himself when others around him were in need. His demeanor was arrogant and boastful, very sure of himself. Know anyone like this? It would probably get under your skin like it would mine.

Listen to how Jesus reacted: "[he] looked at him and loved him" (Mark 10:21).

Read that one more time.

Jesus—looked—at—him—and—loved—him.

Notice that it doesn't say, "Jesus looked at him and was disgusted by the impurity in his heart," or "Jesus looked at him and thought, 'Get me away from this guy!'"

No, Jesus looked at the man and loved him, seeing the world through the lens of grace. And then Jesus gently called him to a hard truth. He knew the idol in this man's heart, and he asked the man to give it up and follow him.

The invitation is the same today. We are called to see those around us through the lens of love and grace. And in community, we are invited to deal with our own idols, our own mess, and sometimes to gently invite others to root out their own idols as well. This doesn't happen through condemnation but through shared invitation.

When we step into the murky waters of Christian community, Christ asks you and me to see beyond the ick and see hearts that were once just little boys or girls infected by this angry, destructive world; to see persons who tried to figure out how to survive their situation and took on some baggage along the way. They are beautiful beneath all that. They are made in the reflection of God. They are hurting, *and* they are loved deeply by Christ.

This isn't always easy. Jesus once gave some strange instructions providing the key to viewing others through his lens of grace. He said: "Love your neighbor as yourself . . ." (Mark 12:31).

Huh? Have you ever considered that the way you view others is just an outflow of the way you view yourself? If you are having difficulty wearing this lens of grace when dealing with others, it's likely because you are still wearing the glasses of judgment toward parts of yourself.

To love others well, you must look at your own brokenness and realize how Christ views you. He sees his son or daughter. He poured out grace on the cross for you, and he pours out daily grace into your life. When he thinks about you, he is filled with joy, brimming with unending patience. When you fail, he is there to pick you up. When you turn away, he is there to lead you back home. When you put on these lenses of self-evaluation, you are enabled to use them to view others with similar results. It becomes impossible to judge them because the branches of grace growing from your spiritual trunk reach outward to them.

In Revelation, the apostle John describes the church as the "bride" of Christ. Every married couple who has withstood the test of time and remains in love knows this: you don't dwell on the wrongs and obvious imperfections of your spouse. You cultivate admiration; you choose to cherish what you can; and you focus first and foremost on improving yourself. This is also how you effectively approach the local church and build Christian community in the process.

If you do, you'll begin to discover a vital secret about all things that are broken; they are mosaic. When shattered pieces are assembled by a skilled artist, they become a breathtaking masterpiece. Though the church you attend is fractured and full of people who have failed and who may fail you (even the pastor or priest), you will find the presence of God in their midst.

How is this possible? Jesus said: "For where two or three gather in my name, there am I with them" (Matthew 18:20).

This could be rewritten, "Where two or three are gathered, there will be a pile of imperfections—rough edges and questionable outcomes—and yet, in the middle, you'll find the living, promised presence of Christ to indwell and transform you. This is the beautiful and broken church, the bride of Christ, into which you are invited. Wrap your mind around that! The presence of Jesus is in the middle of the church mess!

So, follow the advice from Hebrews 10:24–25:

Let us . . . not [give] up meeting together, as some are in the habit of doing, but [encourage] one another—and all the more as you see the Day approaching.

Find a church. Dive in deep. Build community. Expect it to be broken. Be ready for your own disillusionment. Persevere and press on. Look at what's wrong in yourself before spiritually sniping at others. And put on the most powerful vision-wear possible, Jesus's lens of grace. You will find the constant, consistent presence of Christ in the middle of this glorious church mess. Don't miss out on it.

CHAPTER 7

The Forgotten Step

Gaining Jesus often means losing an earthly relationship. For me, that relationship was with my Jewish dad. Let me introduce you to him through a few flashbacks.

There was that time on a family vacation when he wore a short pink bathing suit before short pink bathing suits were cool, especially if you had scrawny, pasty white legs like his. Or when he would dig through our Halloween candy stash and eat all the gross stuff, including black licorice and anything with coconut (sorry if you are a fan of those flavors). Or when he would train for a marathon and I would ride my bike alongside him with our dogs, Erika and Nellie. Or the time he gave me my first Swiss Army pocket knife, oh yeah! There were fishing outings, ice skating afternoons, and canoe trips together.

There were unseen moments when he helped a friend with multiple sclerosis get home from the train station and the grocery store every week but told nobody. And the rainy, Grateful Dead concert he took me to for my twelfth birthday—who does that? He spent all night pushing strangers' vehicles out of calf-deep mud in the parking lot while I slept in the car.

There were the harsh arguments that turned my heart cold. The tantrum I threw by scratching out his face in family photos. My escapism into drugs, anger, and emptiness. The emotional distance over many years that set in, when he disengaged emotionally, relationally, turned to workaholism, and became unavailable. Even though he grew up Jewish, at this point in life he wanted nothing to do with God. It also seemed that, as I grew older, he wanted nothing to do with me.

I interpreted his heart-crushing though never spoken message as: "You are not accepted." Often, in my dad's presence, I felt unseen and deeply misunderstood. For some of those years, we were wholly estranged from each another. Even after I became a Christian, I carried a dull grade of resentment and had a painful void in my life. I ached for connection and belonging with him.

After ten years passed with no changes, I started to hit a wall in my faith that I could not understand. I would try to feel and express the peace of Christ, but instead anxiety and anger would pop to the surface. I would try to reflect on the grace of God but instead felt something sharp was cutting into my soul. As a Christian leader, I tried to be loving to others and instead I struggled to put myself aside and show authentic care. I was using people for my own gain, holding back in relationships, tense, sad, and quickly aggravated. God himself began to seem distant, unapproachable—and I couldn't explain why.

I was not consistently experiencing what I read about in Galatians.

> But the fruit of the Spirit is love, joy, peace, forbearance, kindness, goodness, faithfulness, gentleness and self-control . . .
>
> **—Galatians 5:22–23**

I knew I was saved by Jesus, and I knew I had the promised Spirit of God within, but something wasn't right. Like a sink drain with a nasty hairball stopping the water flow, I had a clog in my faith. I wasn't experiencing all the new life and freedom God had promised. I had a choice: to blame God or to consider that my faith problem might be "user error."

I read Jesus' Sermon on the Mount in Matthew 6, honestly reflecting on these words:

> "For if you forgive other people when they sin against you, your heavenly Father will also forgive you. But if you do not forgive others their sins, your Father will not forgive your sins."
>
> **—Matthew 6:14–15**

This is serious business! For some reason, whenever I thought about the concept of forgiving others, I always considered it a decent idea, kind of like flossing your teeth. I would do it when I thought about it but go months without touching the floss. C'mon! Don't judge me, do you really floss every day? However, right here in this sermon, Jesus places giving forgiveness on par with receiving the forgiveness of God.

He essentially says, "Unforgiveness in your heart will block the flow of the Father's blessing into your life. You can't expect to receive all God has for you and not give that blessing of forgiveness away to others."

It hit me. The clog in the pipes of my faith was real. I thought forgiveness had worked its way into the corners of my soul, but I'd blocked it by holding on to unforgiveness in my past. It became very clear to me; my faith would never progress, certainly not thrive, possibly not even survive, if I did not figure out how to forgive.

I had unconsciously believed the misleading phrase "time heals all wounds," but I was starting to see that that statement may be a dangerous lie. True, time can dull some of our extreme emotions. That dampening might even begin to feel like a version of healing. Time, however, does not always heal. Sometimes time deepens wounds, solidifies malformations, and preserves poisons.

I began to realize the kitschy thought, "whatever doesn't kill you makes you stronger," might be misleading too. What if some experiences don't kill us physically, but rather kill us spiritually,

111

relationally, or emotionally depending on how we handle them? What if Anne Lamott is right when she says, "Not forgiving is like drinking rat poison and then waiting for the rat to die."[1] We are only damaging ourselves.

God began to teach me, if we want to move forward in faith, we must go back and forgive.

Again, when I became a Christian, I thought my new life and new heart meant my old life and my old heart were incapable of affecting me. It wasn't true for me; you will quickly find out it's not true for you either. It is possible and quite common for new Christians to carry the pain of the past into the promised land of their new faith. Then we wonder why the promised land of new life in Christ isn't free of the old hindrances. It's because we brought them there.

Some of the greatest advice I received during those years is summarized by the author Pete Scazzero, who wrote, "Emotional health and spiritual maturity are inseparable. It is not possible to be spiritually mature while remaining emotionally immature." [2]

I had some work to do regarding forgiveness in my life, especially in my relationship with my father. This wasn't going to be easy. Partly because as I learned more about true forgiveness and watched many of my friends attempting to forgive others, I realized many Christians do it all wrong. That might sound a little supercilious. Don't worry, I fully acknowledge I made many messy forgiveness errors along the way and am sure you will face Christian myths and mistakes about forgiveness yourself. Let's tackle these misguided attempts and rebuild a clear plan about how to effectively forgive as Christ commands us.

Forgiveness Mistake #1: Forcing Forgiveness

Sometimes we do to ourselves what we parents often do to our children: force forgiveness just as we force apologies, without doing the work forgiveness requires.

I might say to my son, forcing an apology: "Isaiah, apologize to your sister for hitting her."

With a sneer and the emotional presence of a turtle, he might respond: "I'm sorry."

Then, forcing forgiveness, I might say to my daughter: "Now Isabelle, forgive your brother."

Her reply oozes with sarcasm: "I forgive you."

That's not transformative! We know Christ has commanded forgiveness, but when we force it without doing the behind-the-scenes work, something destructive takes shape. A bitter root of resentment sets in. Rather than peace and freedom from forgiveness, our hearts begin to shut down and close others out, God included. How do we keep this from happening?

If someone has hurt you or disappointed you, the way to forgive fully is to recognize the full cost incurred, the true pain of what has taken place. The depth to which you deal with the real hurt or disappointment is the depth to which forgiveness will take root in your heart. Pretending there is no pain in order to forgive is a guaranteed path to peacelessness.

Said another way, a shallow recognition of the cost will produce shallow, powerless forgiveness.

Sarah leads our kids so well in this. Instead of forcing forgiveness first, she might say, "Sounds like your brother really hurt you. That makes sense; being hit with a Barbie doll hurts. And it sounds like you are really angry about it. Makes sense too. Especially when you just wanted him to play with you, and you feel rejected by him." Now Isabelle is aware of what was really damaged, the depth. So, when she goes to forgive her brother, which she ultimately gets around to, it's not petty or pretend. She's well aware of what the cost was and what she is choosing to forgive.

Such daily kid issues are small-beans forgiveness compared to some of the massive feelings you might need to wade through. My friend Stacey grew up in a family where her feelings weren't valued or validated and where her parents showed strong favoritism toward her brother. She thought she had worked through these issues, until an explosive family dinner brought everything to the surface. Hurts and betrayals that had been rooting deep in her heart for more than thirty years were exposed and she left feeling uncared for, unprotected, and angry. But she tried to put on a nice face and forgive. It didn't work.

Even months after the event she struggled to talk to her parents and started shaking every time she even thought about her brother. One day, she confided in a friend and said, "I don't know what to do; I don't know how to forgive them." Her wise friend told her, "You can't go around those feelings; you have to go through them in order to forgive." So, Stacey gave it a shot, went into a quiet room in her apartment, and screamed into a pillow. She appropriately felt and let out all the anger and hurt she'd been trying to smooth over or ignore. Only after she did just that was she was able to move forward in taking real steps toward forgiving her family.

Forgiveness requires us to go through feelings, not around them. Going around feelings means they are still there, just buried. Through is the only way up and out.

We don't have to do this hard work alone; in fact, we can't. "The LORD is close to the brokenhearted and saves those who are crushed in spirit" (Psalm 34:18).

Going through means we walk with Christ through the anger or sadness or betrayal in order to receive his restoration. We might often think, "Lord, I want to get rid of all the negativity I feel inside, so I can finally experience you." We think it's the pain or emotion inside of us that keeps us from the Lord. But the opposite is true. According to Psalm 34, it's in the middle of hurt where we find the Lord and his power to help us.

If we attempt to avoid the hurt, we inadvertently miss the presence of God who is waiting in the midst of the mess. I don't share these truths lightly. Wounds that need forgiving come in all shapes and sizes. Yours might be considerable, resulting from terrible abuses; or they may be more ordinary, resulting from everyday life frustrations. I am not minimizing your reality, rather I am inviting you to walk toward what seems like the darkness because that is where you will discover the light of Christ.

This will take time and will require help. For all of us, it is the Holy Spirit who can directly provide this help. Through prayer, journaling, and reflection, you can pour out your hurt directly to God, with his presence right there with you. I picture a sponge full of soaked-up pain and hurt. In order to move on, the sponge needs to be wrung out until every last drop of the hurt has been expressed into the ocean of God's love.

The Spirit's power is thorough and always ready to meet us in the mess. However, God also provides friends, loved ones, and professional counselors to walk this path, as needed. Don't hesitate to lean into any of these resources. I did, and I still do.

Just remember, forgiveness isn't flippant. We must do the behind-the-scenes work forgiveness requires. We have to acknowledge and walk through the depth of the hurt to experience the depth of forgiveness. True forgiveness doesn't pretend; it faces and feels the pain of the past in the presence of God.

Forgiveness Mistake #2: Equating Forgiveness with Reconciliation

Many people equate forgiveness with reconciliation and paralyze progress with both. What do I mean? Forgiveness is necessary for reconciliation but far from identical. Let's first get clear on the definition of those two terms.

Forgiveness means canceling a debt. It means letting go of the idea that you deserve something in return from another person. Forgiveness says, "You don't owe me anything anymore." That's it. As we just discussed, this doesn't minimize the effect of the relational debt or wound left behind; it just means there will no longer be expectation of repayment. There's no more "eye for an eye."

Here's the irony about forgiveness: in choosing to let the other person off the hook (because that's what God has done for us through Jesus), it's actually letting yourself off the hook from bitter resentment. Giving forgiveness is giving a gift to yourself—choosing to no longer believe you are incomplete until someone pays you back in some way; choosing to no longer act the victim at the mercy of the person who once hurt you. God tells us we are complete, needing nothing other than him to be whole, because he has offered us his forgiveness.

If you choose not to forgive but rather hold on to the grudge, you choose to put all the power into the hands of the person who hurt you. By choice, you are letting that person's leftover wound define you rather than letting the forgiveness of Christ define you. The moment you choose to forgive and let go of the debt, you take the power back from the other person and return it to the hands of Christ.

You then have the power to be free, to be healed through the work of the Spirit, and to grow no matter what the person did or didn't do to you.

I sometimes wonder if Christ's strict command to forgive (the Matthew 6 reference I mentioned earlier in the chapter) was less about a harsh punishment if we don't forgive and more about Jesus recognizing that non-forgiveness naturally causes an internal disintegration within us.

■ ■ ■

Reconciliation goes much further than forgiveness. It means wrongs have been made right *and* the relationship is restored. Friendship, love, trust, and ongoing communication are back in full force. Reconciliation is a return to the way the relationship once was or even a strengthening into what it can be. This is where confusing reconciliation and forgiveness causes a numbing breakdown.

You might be thinking, "Reconciliation is a tall order. I don't think I can ever enter back into a relationship with so-and-so because of what they did or the character I know they possess." Maybe that's true. You've implemented Ephesians 4:3, "Make every effort to keep the unity of the Spirit through the bond of peace." And still there is no visible hope of reconciliation. Or maybe the person in question was abusive, untrustworthy, or no longer living, so reconciliation becomes unadvisable or impossible.

In one sense, this is okay for your journey of forgiveness. It's neither ideal nor God's original plan. However, we must remember, forgiveness and reconciliation are different. Reconciliation is a *goal* to strive for, but forgiveness is a *command* of Christ we must fulfill. After choosing to forgive someone, you may then begin a process of reconciliation. Or you may need to keep strict boundaries in place—unless or until something drastically changes in that relationship.

It is possible to forgive and *not* reconcile and still fulfill the command of Christ. Don't let the weight of reconciliation or the fear of needing to reenter a terribly destructive relationship prevent you from choosing to forgive. You will be fulfilling the command of Christ and releasing yourself from a bondage you do not need in your life.

Forgiveness Mistake #3: Waiting for an Apology

You might be thinking, "Don't you need to have a conversation with the other person in order to fully forgive? Don't they need to apologize or make amends or 'own their stuff'? Does it take two to tango or is giving forgiveness really just an individual sport?" This may seem like minutia, but it really is a faith-shaping detail.

If we can't talk it out with someone for whatever reason, are we the ones stuck with the peacelessness and bitter root of unforgiveness?

We don't have to be. Forgiveness is a choice we make alone; it's between us and God. It does not require an exchange between us and the person who caused the offense. This might be new, breakthrough information for you; it was for me. There's no need to hold on to it any longer, waiting for the other person to come around. Forgiveness is up to you and you alone. How do you do this? By confronting the next mistake.

Forgiveness Mistake #4: Keeping Something Alive That Should Die

We often forget this vital forgiveness truth: something must die in order to forgive (Brené Brown).[3] I know it sounds morbid, but

117

remember, forgiveness in a relationship means the end of something that we've been carrying. We must first let go of the debt created by releasing the right to be repaid in some way. But beyond that, we must choose to let go of something else.

Maybe it's an expectation—a dream we've had that the relationship would go in a certain direction. We have to accept that the relationship may not materialize the way we'd hoped. Then we must do the work forgiveness requires and let the expectation die.

Maybe it's our view of the other person that we need to let die. Maybe we've idealized them, creating an image they can never live up to. Or maybe it's the opposite. We've smeared them in our minds, demonizing them and thinking their intentions and motives are entirely negative. The reality, of course, is they aren't all bad or all good, but a mix of both. They are trying to do the very best they can with the inner resources they have to draw upon. We need to see that they are broken and imperfect just like us.

We will have to let some things die for forgiveness to take root. This is the work of God the Father, who allowed his own Son to die so forgiveness could be possible. In receiving his forgiveness, we step into the circle of people, following after their Father in heaven, who are committed to always-only-ever forgive; people who understand true forgiveness always requires the death of something of great value.

Forgiveness Mistake #5: Letting Something Die Which Should Stay Alive

One final mistake when it comes to forgiveness is letting something die that we never should. So often, we give up hope. Don't! Hold on to hope!

Hang on to a "you-never-know-what-can-happen" spirit. What if God can change their heart? What if God can change *your* heart? What if God can change your relationship?

What if on the other side of the bitterness is complete freedom? Certainly, there is freedom from the toxins which forgiveness leaves in your life. But there could also be the blessing of friendships and families restored, words spoken and received that you never could have imagined. What if when Christ's command to forgive is fulfilled, it releases more power and potential for the Spirit of God to change a life, to change a situation? What if when you walk through the threshold of forgiveness, the clogs in your faith fade away? What if you discover more power from the Spirit of God and more of his intimate presence in your daily life than you ever imagined? "Let us hold unswervingly to the hope we profess, for he who promised is faithful" (Hebrews 10:23).

What does "holding on to hope" look like for you?

To start the forgiveness journey, you don't need to hold to a vision of reconciled relationship; you just need to know you can't be free without forgiveness. Holding on to hope for you might mean jumping back into the past to deal with an undealt area of your life. It will mean trusting that God will be close to you throughout the process; you may unravel a bit, but he will reweave your heart by his Spirit. You will be emptied of the inner toxic sludge which wants to take over your future.

Holding on to hope might mean to keep asking God for the relationship back. For the friendship to strengthen. For the family member to be reconciled. Forgiveness is certainly the oft-forgotten step. God might do what only God can do and give you what you've been longing to see. In order for that to happen, you must first choose to do what only you can do and follow the command of Christ: forgive.

■ ■ ■

Holding on to hope was the critical final step in my journey of forgiveness with my father as I walked into his hospice room.

There was no ticking clock on the wall. There were no beeps from machines and monitors. This sterile room was designed for quiet, for letting go. Close to a decade of fighting Parkinson's had ruined my dad's mind and body. Only the occasional twitch from his closed eyelids, a whisper of breath, and a vaguely rising chest showed signs of remaining life. Everyone was about to leave to catch a flight. We had waited for many days, but beneath the failing figure, he still hung on, silently saying, "I'm not quite ready yet."

I stepped toward my dad's bed, opened my hand, palm facing down, and affectionately placed it on his chest. I felt the warmth and a faint heartbeat resonate through the thin hospital gown. He'd been physically unresponsive for almost two weeks. With my hand over his heart for only a split second, his crusted eyelids shot open. I jumped backward. (You would too!) Then, I leaned in close to his face. He couldn't move. His pupils dilated and contracted until he focused on me. His mouth twitched with great effort, trying to smile. My words felt like putting on a perfectly worn pair of old gloves.

"I love you so much. I'm so proud to call you my dad. Dad, I am so thankful for the love you gave and showed me. I learned so much from you: how to show compassion and care for people, how to be diligent and softhearted. I love you, I love you, I love you." His eyes reddened and filled with tears. Then I said, "Dad, as I'm a pastor now, I want you to know you are at peace. You are in the hands of a God who loves you. When you trusted in Jesus, he promised to forgive you, to restore you to God, and to welcome you home." Then I read Psalm 23 to him and finished with its closing words, "You, Dad, will dwell in the house of the Lord forever."

My sister and my mom and the grandkids all came in after that and each had a sweet moment of final words as time stood still. Then he slowly passed away. I loved him with the fullest love I can imagine.

Sounds a little different than what I described at the beginning of this chapter, doesn't it? Years earlier, I fought hard to confront the mistakes and discover each of the forgiveness lessons I mentioned. I knew forgiveness couldn't be flippant, and I felt the pain of a distant dad, the anger of broken promises that left their arrows in me. But I realized I needed to do business with God alone, to get my needs met through him; to choose to forgive my dad without being able to talk through all the issues with him.

Eventually, I began to see my dad as human again, not just the guy who irreparably ticked me off. I let him off the hook in my heart, no longer requiring any repayment or apology—knowing, in fact, he probably couldn't provide any of that for me anyway. I let my impossible expectations of Dad die, along with my skewed image of who he was and wasn't.

I had a particular moment with a group of friends when I drew "a line in the sand," stepped over it, and said, "I now choose to forgive my dad." Over time, as the hurts subsided, they were replaced with prayers for my dad. "God, bring my dad to you," I asked over and over again. And he did.

One day before my father lost his lucidity, we had an unforgettable moment together. I sensed the Holy Spirit nudging me to say to him, "Dad, we've talked about setting up power of attorney for your health and physical matters because you know you can't take care of yourself any longer. It's time now to set up power of attorney for your soul to Jesus. He is the only one who can take care of your spiritual needs, to make you right with God." How else do you explain the gospel of God's hope and forgiveness through Christ to an old Jewish lawyer?

Not only did he trust in Jesus, he also broke down crying and spoke the words of blessing to me that every son wants to hear from his father: "I'm proud of you, Craig. I couldn't be prouder of who you've become as a man. I'm proud of what you are doing with your life. I not only love you deeply, I respect you. You are a great man."

That was my dad! The one whom I had lost all hope in. The one whose heart was closed to God for over seventy years, the one whom I resented and hardly related to for almost twenty years. Amazing! What could have been a story of a broken relationship, bitterness, and an empty, estranged life ending is now a story of complete redemption. I spoke every possible blessing to my dad before he passed away, and I meant it. He spoke every blessing to me and meant it. We had forgiven one another and reconciled as well. Everything changed.

CHAPTER 8

The Final Flaw

W hen I was a teenager, I engaged in an extracurricular, long-term "borrowing" activity from a local store. It was more about the rebel child's rush of dangerous adventure than the desperation for a loaf of bread like Jean Valjean in *Les Misérables*. I stole a purple Patagonia belt. Laugh at me all you want; this was during my hippie, granola, Grateful Dead, go-camping-every-weekend phase.

I wore that purple wonder belt for years. Until one day, well after I became a Christian. I was reading Ephesians 6:

Put on the breastplate of righteousness . . .
Okay, got it.
the belt of truth . . .
Yep, uh-huh.
and take up the sword of the Spirit which is the word of God.
Wait a minute. What was that? Belt of who?

I glanced down at my purple sash. "Belt of truth, oh no . . . [You have to read this with a bit of overdramatized exaggeration.] Oh my goodness, I'm not wearing the belt of truth, I'm wearing the belt of sin! Take it off! Take it off! Take it off!"

"Maybe," I thought, "I got all the answers wrong on the final exam because I've been wearing a cursed, stolen belt! Or, maybe when I broke my wrist playing indoor soccer it had something to do with the belt!"

Actually, I got the answers wrong on my final because I didn't study. And I broke my wrist because I was a crazy man on the field and fell, *not* because I wore a voodoo sin belt and was being punished by God for it. To be clear, Jesus has taken the punishment for all our sins—past, present, and future—on the cross. God is not punishing us for them. That's not how God works.

Even so, natural and even supernatural consequences to sin may remain—such as a lack of peace, a carried sense of guilt, an estrangement from others, a perceived distance from God, inner emptiness, and limited blessing flowing through our lives. And, depending on the wrong that has been done, there are real-world practical damages too—like broken cars, broken families, and broken memories.

Back to my belt. I took it off, threw it across my college dorm room, and prayed a confession: "God, I stole this belt. I am so sorry! Please forgive me. I don't even like purple anymore. Please let me put on the belt of truth instead, whatever that means." And that was that. Sin confessed, belt removed, end of story. I thought.

I went out and bought (not stole) a new belt: I stepped up to braided, light-brown leather. Yeah, this was still the '90s. I wore the new belt proudly: "No belt of sin here. Just a good ol' braided belt." Life went on for another six months.

But then I came across a verse in James 5 during a time of 4Step Scripture reading: "Therefore confess your sins one to each other . . . so that you may be healed" (James 5:16).

I read the text again. It was pretty clear. I tried to understand the context. James (the author) was talking to a young Middle Eastern church full of new believers who needed to understand what was at the core of handling sin. Equally clear.

Identifying the principle wasn't difficult either.

Confess your sins to one another . . .
　　"Okay, got that."
　　. . . so that you may be healed.

"Wait. I thought we confess our sins to God so that we may be healed. What's this to-one-another deal? That doesn't jive with the whole 'my faith is a personal thing' philosophy at all. Is this really saying what I think it is saying?"

Scripture pronounces that when we confess our sins to God we are forgiven. This is as clear as a backcountry trout stream. But Scripture then declares that forgiveness isn't all we need. The next move requires more than God alone. Catch that?

I had to take this principle and make it personal. Remember: studying the Bible and filling your head with a bunch of self-help principles but not applying them to your life is like studying exercise while sitting on the couch eating Twinkie Pie and finishing your fourth pack of cigarettes of the day. It doesn't get you very far. I have no idea what Twinkie Pie is by the way, but it sounds disgusting.

"God," I prayed. "How do you want me to make this principle personal? How do you want me to respond and apply this truth to my life?" As I continued, I looked up and in the corner of my dorm room floor lay that stinking purple belt. My heart sank. The darned belt of sin was still lingering in my life.

"That silly thing? I confessed that wrongdoing six months ago."

Oh, wait, one to another?

"You mean you want me to tell a friend I stole the belt. Okay, no big deal."

No, that's not it? Who did I sin against?

"Well, you, God. But I guess, well, I guess the shop owner too."

No! You can't be serious?

"You want me to go back to the shop owner whom I stole from three years ago? Oh my God! Oh wait, that's you. Oh my goodness, I mean."

■ ■ ■

Winter break was conveniently two weeks away, so I could go home and stop by the shop where I stole the belt. By this time, I was dating Sarah, my lovely wife now and my awesome girlfriend back then. I told her my plan and asked for her help.

"Sarah, you come into the store with me and tell the shop owner what I did and that I'm sorry. I'll just stand there, okay?"

"Ha!" she said. "You're funny, Craig. Get in there and take ownership for what you did."

So, I walked in and immediately noticed the guy who owned the shop. He was right there behind the counter. He smiled kindly at me. I was sure beneath the smile he was thinking I was a petty thief and planning another attack on his merchandise, or at least that's the story I told myself. I meandered around for a few minutes, shuffling through items, pretending I was going to make a purchase. My heart was racing; my hands were sweaty. I didn't know a twenty-five-dollar mistake would be so overwhelming! Finally, the customer whom the owner had been talking to left, and it was just the owner and me in the store. This was the perfect opportunity.

He came over to me and said, "Can I help you with anything?"

"No, thanks," I said, and I instantly turned around and walked-ran out of the store. I'm serious. I bolted on my mission!

I came back to the car, got inside, and told Sarah, "I chickened out; I couldn't do it. This is too difficult!"

She didn't say anything, but she looked back at me with those eyes.

I took a deep breath, opened the door, and went back into the store. The owner looked at me with a funny "What's up?" I had clearly made everything more awkward than it needed to be and he could tell I was shaking and nervous.

I opened my mouth and spit out about five words per second. "I'm so sorry, sir. My name is Craig and a few years ago I came into your store with my friends and I stole this purple belt from you. [I pulled the belt out of a bag.] I have felt terrible about it, really. Since then, I've made peace with God, and following him is what my life is all about. Now I want to make peace with you. I'm sorry I stole your belt; I'm here to give it back to you and pay you for it as well."

"Wow, young man," he said. "I know people have stolen from me, but no one has ever come back and apologized. That means a lot. Well, you keep on that good path and keep the belt too; it's my gift to you. I forgive you."

I walked out of his store in joyful, free-hearted tears. I literally felt a sensation of heaviness and guilt melt off my shoulders. There was a healing in my heart and what felt like a layer of gunk removed from my soul. Yes, I was already ultimately forgiven by God, but I experienced a new level of healing which comes through confession to another. I celebrated with Sarah. And then, I whipped the ugly braided leather belt off my belt loops and put my old purple mainstay back on. It was no longer the belt of sin. Now it was the belt of truth! The belt declared in all its purpleness the truth that God has forgiven me through Christ and given me life to the full as a gift. That belt announced redemption. It became a reminder literally wrapped around my body.

As we confess Christ as our king, we are forgiven, *and* as we confess wrongs to others, we are healed and so are our relationships. This is powerful stuff. It will change your life like it did mine. You might even start wearing purple belts.

The Crossroad of Hiding or Confessing

Let's unpack this. Even in Christ, we are flawed. Since you and I have a 100 percent chance of not being perfect, we need a strategy to manage our mistakes. There are really only two options. Every mistake creates a crossroads where we either choose to confess or to conceal.

We understand the meaning of concealing: it's hiding from reality. Concealing is when we avoid our mistakes, pretend they aren't there, minimize them, blame and explain around them. Unfortunately, concealing only allows mistakes to multiply. The negative effects then compound and retain more control over our lives. It's like a splinter beneath the skin; it will eventually lead to infection and constant pain unless it is pulled out. Concealing never leads to healing; concealing cuts off relationship and stunts growth.

What about the other option, confession?

The verb "to confess" in biblical Greek can also translate as "to agree." Confession is agreeing with reality. It means we acknowledge what is true. It requires avoiding half-truths, mixed messages, and hidden details. Confession is a refresh back to factory settings. Isn't it a relief when you've messed up your mobile phone, to just revert back and undo the software damage? Or to use another analogy, confession feels like escaping a riptide. If you try to swim straight against the current by concealing reality, you'll exhaust yourself and drown. If the riptide is strong enough, you can't even swim sideways to get out of the current. The best solution could be to agree with reality: to confess. Calm down and allow the riptide to carry you just past the swell of waves where the current weakens, and you can emerge in safer waters.

Misconceptions about Confession

Unfortunately, Christians have often taught an incomplete model of confession which cripples its power. The idea is that every mistake we make is ultimately against God, which is true. God created life in all its perfection and beauty; any damage to life goes against the gift and the intentions of God. So, if we want to cut to the chase and go to the source, every time we do something wrong, we should just confess to God. This part is accurate. We should never withhold anything from God; we should always confess directly to him.

And yes, he already knows everything about us. He's the omniscient (all-knowing) God, after all. But for the sake of our relationship, he wants us to bring it to the surface of our communication with him. It's sort of like a child who scribbled with crayons on the wall. If the child pretends as though she didn't do it or lies and blames it on someone else (even if she signed it "Art by Isabelle"—not like that's ever happened in my home!), this will cause damage to the relationship. The parent wants open honesty, and the child can only grow in character with pure acknowledgment of the truth.

Confession to God is vital. The moment you are aware of wrongdoing, bring it to your good and loving Father in heaven. And you can memorize Romans 8:1 to remind you of the truth that . . . "Therefore, there is now no condemnation for those who are in Christ Jesus."

No condemnation! Whatever you bring to your Father in heaven is forgiven. Jesus paid the price for it on the cross, and he was raised to new life. Acknowledging Jesus as your leader and forgiver applies his work of salvation to your life. This means the moment you confess to God in private, you are free from shame. You are united with him.

But, please let this sink in: confession to God alone is not only incomplete, it's not biblical. Biblical confession always involves another person. Throughout Scripture, private sins were shared appropriately with others. We see this concept clearly throughout the laws of the Old Testament. Confession always involved apologizing to any person who was wronged and making amends. We likewise see person-to-person confession in the early church period after Christ was resurrected (see the book of Acts). Having a secret conversation with God in the face of wrongdoing never cut it in the Scriptures and never led to the healing of the heart and the mending of broken relationships.

If you peek into church history, you'll discover a common thread among all the great awakenings, times when hundreds of thousands of people were swept up into new relationship with Jesus. Outpourings of God's favor always begin with an outpouring of humble confession to each other.

Confess to God for forgiveness. Confess to others for healing.

If we want the healing and favor of God and if we want lasting connection in our relationships, we must learn how to overcome our fatal flaws through confession. We must learn to push back the temptation to conceal and begin admitting reality in the midst of our community.

Don't worry, I'm not about to ask you to stand up during a crowded church service and shout your deepest darkest at the top of your lungs and then sit down as if nothing happened. That's just weird. But I do want to get very practical with you.

A Practical Approach to Confession

First, there are two different types of confession. One is when we confess something that appears private. We feel the wrong was an act that didn't outright hurt another person or break a commitment. We feel the sin is between ourselves and God alone. I won't spend much time on this here, but think back to the analogy of the aspen tree grove. If you keep making private mistakes and only sharing them with God, you'll end up isolated and powerless when what you need is strength from a root system of integrated community. Take a risk; find someone you can trust who will hold your confidence, someone who is following Jesus with abandon, and share reality with them. Ask them to remind you of God's truth and help you create a plan of growth.

However, you'll discover most of our flaws hardly occur in a private vacuum. There are direct and indirect effects of our wrongs on others. Think of it as throwing a small stone that creates a ripple effect on the still water.

I'm sure we've all seen celebrities or politicians who appear on television to make half-hearted, insincere apologies for betraying the public trust. In contrast, have you ever received a genuinely honest apology from someone who is willing to take ownership for the effects of their actions? It's like warm sunshine breaking through on a dark day. It is healing for all involved. It creates immediate respect. It diffuses tension. It rebuilds trust. It's the soil for repaired friendship. It is a reflection of heaven on earth.

True, apologies alone can be empty (we will get to that), but I've found our world is losing the art of apology and replacing it with destructive deflection, blame, and fear-fueled concealment. We need to regain this invaluable skill for the sake of our faith and for the sake of our society.

Dr. Gary Chapman and Jennifer Thomas have written an insightful book titled *The Five Languages of Apology*.[1] Here's a crash course in his framework for effective apology, in my own words. Master the five steps for your own healing.

1. Express Regret

Consider the three magic words, "I am sorry." International conflicts have become entrenched, couples have gone to divorce court, and friends have ended decades of camaraderie for lack of these three genuine words. They are possibly the most powerful words we can learn to say.

But not always. You have received an empty apology, right? You know how vacuous it feels. My kids do it. "I'm sorry," they say. But what they really want is to appease their overbearing dad and return to watching their show. Adults give empty "I'm sorrys" too, often in a more sophisticated manner. "Mistakes were made; I'm sorry you felt that way; I'm sorry that bothered you"—all are attempts at deflecting and dismissing rather than taking heartfelt ownership.

How do we ensure we don't say empty "I'm sorrys" to each other? By adding three additional, essential letters when expressing regret:

F-O-R

Whenever beginning an apology say, "I am sorry **for** . . ." Get specific and even explain the upsetting effect your actions likely had on the other person.

"I'm sorry *for* showing up late when I told you I'd be here on time. I know that caused you a lot more stress." That's a decent apology.

"I'm sorry *for* belittling your idea in front of those people. I can see I hurt you." Or, "I'm sorry *for* not listening to you intently and making the conversation primarily about me. I was insensitive."

Always add the FOR. Those hurt by your actions will feel validated, heard, noticed, and tension will immediately soften.

You can still ruin your apology at this point by adding three more letters:

B-U-T

"I'm sorry for missing your game, *but* something came up at work."

"I'm sorry for not listening well, *but* you were really talking a lot."

"I'm sorry for sleeping around, *but* you were never there for me."

Can you hear how *but* destroys the apology? It makes excuses. It minimizes the recognition of your wrong; it subtly shifts blame; it creates an empty apology.

I'll make this easy for us to remember. Never show your butt when apologizing! My ten-year-old son wanted me to add that. Now for the next step:

2. Accept Responsibility

This might cut to the bone. Do you realize how your body literally fights against saying, "I was wrong"? Try it. Go ahead. Out loud in full voice say, "I was wrong." C'mon, humor me.

Okay, now say it one more time. "I was wrong."

How did that feel? Awkward. Painful. Unnatural. It's as if there is a hard disk program in our heads which prevents our tongue from forming those words.

Why? It's called good-bad, right-wrong, black-and-white thinking, which assumes if we admit to being wrong in some small way that we are completely wrong and the only wrongdoer.

Dr. John Townsend[2] has established that one of the indicators of adulthood and emotional/spiritual maturity is the ability to hold both good and bad at the same time, in tension.

If we discover we are wrong in some way, it doesn't automatically mean we are wrong about everything. We can be partly wrong and partly right at the same time. It's not an indictment on our whole person to say, "I was wrong." It's just an ability to acknowledge the reality that I'm a little bit right and a little bit wrong and not crumble under that truth.

In the context of an apology, saying you are wrong doesn't mean the other person isn't wrong in some way either. It just means for this apology, you are willing to own your part, even if your part isn't all that went wrong in the situation.

Like most siblings, my children sometimes fight. And at times they need to apologize for hurtful things they've said to one another. When my son acknowledges something hurtful he said to his sister, and takes ownership for that, it doesn't mean that she didn't also say something hurtful to him. Or perhaps they are arguing about whether something is true or not; he says it isn't and she says it is. He can be making the right, or correct, point but making it in a way that is wrong and hurtful. He can accept responsibility for being hurtful and approaching the situation in a way he shouldn't have, without it meaning that he wasn't right in the point he was making.

You can't control how the other person will respond, but you can set the tone by owning your part first. When all is settled, you are held accountable for yourself alone.

Saying "What I did was somewhat self-centered; I was mostly concerned about my needs at the time," doesn't mean we are defined as a selfish person, and it doesn't mean the person we are talking to doesn't also sometimes make self-centered choices. It just means we are owning our part.

Saying "I was wrong" will transform our apologies and pave the way toward powerful healing. Now for the next step . . .

3. Make Restitution: "What Can I Do to Make It Right?"

This is another area where we often get biblical confession wrong. We receive God's eternal grace and forgiveness, but we forget that our flaws create human costs and tangible consequences.

Jesus once encountered a greedy and deceitful guy named Zacchaeus. Zacchaeus embezzled everyone he did business with and stole from the poor. By grace he was ultimately forgiven by Christ. However, part of Zacchaeus's confession included making things right to those he'd wronged. Zacchaeus committed to go back to the poor, apologize to them directly, and pay back up to four times what he had taken. Jesus seemed to appreciate Zacchaeus's response and blessed his efforts of restitution.

This same principle applies to us. Although we are forgiven by God, if we have created a debt in a relationship, we need to make things right if we want to be healed. I learned this lesson with my purple belt. Biblical confession and apology include making things right to those we've wronged. Next . . .

4. Genuinely Repent: "I'll Work to Not Do That Again"

What happens if someone takes all the right steps in apology up to this point and says, "I'm sorry. I was wrong. How can I make it right?" but they never change their actions.

It starts to become cheap, fake, manipulative—more damaging than before the apology. Repentance is the biblical concept of admitting our wrong *and* changing our direction. The word "repentance" translates as "to change course." Repentance means we stop doing what we have been doing *and* start doing what we need to be doing. Genuine repentance leads to genuine change.

Here's a serious example to illustrate the point: pornography. Pornography is creating an insidious and widespread addiction to destructive sexual images and behaviors in our world, in our schools, in our churches, and in our relationships. You may struggle with this yourself.

In a marriage, pornography is not a private sin. Even though it might be viewed privately, it is a direct offense against a spouse and against a marriage commitment. If we commit to follow James 5:16 and if we want to be healed, then we need to confess both to God and to one another, even with pornography. This especially includes apologizing directly to all those who have been hurt by that wrong, particularly a spouse. I know that is challenging news to some.

Addressing this flaw in an apology would include every step we've discussed.

"I'm sorry, I was wrong, and I want to make things right. And here's my plan to work toward not doing that again . . ." For the repentance to be genuine, the behavior needs to change. Here are some ways to include actions into your apologetic repentance in this example.

You might commit to a no-secrets marriage. Any and every time you cross a line again, you commit to share that with your spouse (which is a helpful and strong deterrent to guide you toward change by the way). Or, maybe you also install a firewall and site-reporting service where your spouse or a friend receives reports on what you view. Or, maybe you also commit to turning off cable TV and staying off the computer by 10 p.m. because that's usually when you slip up. Or, maybe you also commit to going to a recovery program at a local church.

You get the point: a genuine apology requires genuine repentance which requires genuine change; otherwise the apology will be a façade.

Alright. Last item in our apology crash course.

5. Request Forgiveness: "Will You Please Forgive Me?"

It is humbling to request forgiveness because it requires relinquishing control. It shows you truly want the relationship restored; it reiterates you know you've wronged the relationship in some way, and there is a cost to that wrong.

Keep in mind this is a request, not a demand. We aren't entitled to be forgiven in our relationships with people, but hopefully we will be. It might take some time or some additional conversation before others can forgive us. That's okay. We don't want to be given forced forgiveness.

▦ ▦ ▦

The five steps can work together in an effective apology, the following being one example I am very practiced in:

> I'm sorry for the way I spoke to you. It was harsh and insensitive. You didn't deserve that, and I was wrong. I'd like to make it up to you and try again to respond in a kind way. Will you please forgive me?

That can be a simple but powerful and effective apologetic confession. It expresses regret, accepts responsibility, offers restitution, shows genuine repentance, and seeks forgiveness. But this apology is only powerful if it is sincere. Following these steps won't magically make an insincere apology sincere. You must be willing to do the heart work that goes along with it. That's up to you.

If we truly want to overcome our flaws, we must learn to confess rather than conceal. This is the only way to be healed. "Therefore confess your sins one to each other . . . so that you may be healed" (James 5:16).

There's Something Still Missing, Part 2: The Dangers of the Dead Sea

Almost no living organism can survive in the Dead Sea (hence the name!). There are no fish, no Loch Ness monsters, no birds hunting for dinner along its shores—nothing except for a few bacterial traces. Nutrients from the sunlight cannot penetrate its hyper-salinized waters. Oxygen cannot breathe its life into the ecosystem. Sure, floating in it makes for a great travel selfie. And the minerals are convenient for ancient Egyptian mummification and other such standard, "daily" uses. But as for the circle of life, the Dead Sea has nothing to offer.

Bodies of water are intended to feed life into the planet. They are supposed to enrich the lands around them and create an environment teeming with the building blocks of DNA, but not the Dead Sea.

Do you know why? Is it because of contaminants from six-thousand-plus years of civilization in that area? Is it because of nuclear testing nearby? Is it because God was angry about all the wars fought in that region, so he smote their water supply? No and no and no.

The Dead Sea is dead because it is both mega-rich in minerals and landlocked. The waters from the Jordan River flow *into* the

Dead Sea, but there is no outflow. Over millennia, minerals have built up and created a noxious, toxic, overfed lake which chokes out any organism.

So it can be with you and me. We are intended to be sources of life to the world around us. This requires both an inflow *and* an outflow: receiving the rich minerals and nutrients from God and pouring out blessing and enrichment to all those he places in our paths.

God's original promise to his people found in Genesis 12 made this clear. "I will bless you . . . so that all peoples on earth will be blessed through you."

So-that! God pours his life into you *so that* you will be an instrument of life to others. God pours his presence into you *so that* you will bring his presence to those who are desperately dry. God pours his grace into you *so that* you will dispense grace to people suffering under the burden of shame. God pours his resources into you *so that* you will enrich those in need. God blesses you *so that* you will be a blessing.

Never allow your faith to become landlocked. Receiving from God can feel like floating on water and makes for a great Instagram post, but it will toxify your soul if there is no outflow. Do not become like the Dead Sea. You are alive, and God has work for you to do in this world. Move with me into these next chapters, where you'll discover paradigm-altering twists on this truth.

CHAPTER 9

A Surprising Equation

God is a remarkable mathematician; he invented math! But in his kingdom not all equations are created equal; I'll explain.

Jesus once sent his guys out for a couple of weeks or so to do some Jesus work. They went village to village on foot (no Segways or full-suspension, fat-tire mountain bikes back then). They brought no extra rations, no phone chargers, no Clif Bars, no cozy wool socks for the end of the evening by the fire. Wherever they visited they were completely dependent on the hospitality of the hosts. This required great faith. Day after day, they tried out their new speeches about Christ, attempted new prayers for sick people, stared down evil, and called upon the power of God, wondering if any of it would work. Guess what, it did! At the end of their initial Boy-Scout-patch-earning operation, they rallied back together with Jesus. They were too tired for high-fives this time.

Jesus was kind when they returned. " . . . Come with me by yourselves to a quiet place and get some rest" (Mark 6:31). How sweet those words must have sounded to the disciples. *Yes, please!*

So, they boarded a boat (even better) and sailed to the far shores. The disciples were probably dreaming of Palestinian piña coladas, fish tacos, and some slow jazz. But something went wrong. They started to hear the faint rumble of footsteps. Then they saw a cloud of dust around the bend along with the muffled sounds of a large crowd; hordes of people had followed them. Oh no, no more trip to Margaritaville! Instead, the energy-draining pleas of people who wanted teaching and prayer and healing. The disciples were spent, likely enraged on the inside but forcing strained smiles to Jesus on the outside.

"This is a remote place," they said, twisting their motives, "and it's already very late. Send the people away so that they can go to the surrounding countryside and villages and buy themselves something to eat."

I'm thinking, "Sure, guys. You're concerned about the welfare of the people." No judgment from me, though; I've been there too. It's like when I want to get the kids to bed early because *they* are tired, and not because I want some "me time" on Netflix.

Jesus knew what was going on and said, "You give them something to eat."

Here's how I imagine the rest of the conversation. "Uh, Jesus, we just told you there's no food here. There's not even a snack shop in this town! Plus, don't you realize it would take a year's salary just to pay for one meal? That can't possibly be a wise use of money. We don't have enough."

Resolute, Jesus said, "What do you have?"

"Hardly anything!" the disciples may have answered. "Just these few loaves and a couple small fish. But that's our dinner, and yours too, Jesus. Besides it's not enough to feed our own tired bodies. We could eat ten times that amount. Don't forget, we were just out doing your work in your name after you sent us. Can't we just eat our pita and fish sticks and not worry about others for a night?"

Jesus likely drew in a pensive breath. He instructed them to have the massive crowd sit down in orderly groups. With grumbling bellies and complete reluctance, the disciples handed over their share. Jesus broke the bread, gave thanks to God the Father, and started distributing the food.

I can't possibly understand the physics of the next moments. As the disciples were handing away their dinner, the food *never ran out!* They just kept giving and giving and giving, an endless supply. All the people (over five thousand), including the weary disciples, ate until they were satisfied. Then, get this, they collected leftovers—twelve baskets full of food! Sometimes when we are running low on ice cream and my kids beat me to it, I wish I could experience a similar miracle. Bottomless cookies and cream for all!

This is impossible, you might think. Molecular biology does not work like this. What exists is what exists. A few loaves of bread and fish do not feed thousands of people with leftovers for the road. Uh uh. Not in this world.

But there is more power at play in this world than we can comprehend. In God's kingdom, miracles happen; because in God's kingdom, his favorite equation is multiplication. When God is involved, one plus one doesn't always equal two. Two fish plus five loaves can equal thousands of meals—plus leftovers! This is part of God's strategy for bringing the wonders of heaven to earth.

This is exciting, right? But not everything multiplies. There are barriers to miraculous multiplication and critical components we must bring to pave the way for these heavenly equations.

Divine Math, Step 1: Change Your Pronouns

Imagine the options at God's disposal to multiply the food. I suppose Jesus could have said "hocus-pocus" and the bread could have appeared from nothing. The Holy Spirit could have internally taken away the hunger pains of the crowds and rejuvenated their bodies with a heavenly-electrolyte, protein-infused invisible bodily process. Or, there could have been a divinely appointed rainstorm at the perfect moment, the clouds could have opened up and dropped baked goods from the sky, driving all the weather reporters crazy. Cue *Cloudy with a Chance of Meatballs* imagery.

Instead, Christ, knowing he was about to turn this seaside meadow into a Lollapalooza-like feast, turned to his disciples and said, "What do you have?" He didn't let them blame-shift or point fingers or walk away from the need; he looked them in the eyes and asked, "What do you have?"

Divine math often looks like this:

Natural resources released + supernatural strength received = multiplied miracle

Imagine this equation in a contemporary setting. We have because God has given, period. Yes, you may have a decent apartment, car, and career because you studied in school and turned that project in on time. You worked hard and treated people fairly along the way and now you can afford at least your basic necessities, if not more. Don't overlook, though, the family you were born into, the brain you utilize, the body you depend on, the beneficial circumstances out of your control, even the air you breathe each and every day are gifts from God. All we stand on, all we depend on, even life itself, is a gift from God.

When we trust in Jesus, we are bought with a price. The price was his life, and as Christians we now declare, "God, we are yours."

This is no small statement. To admit, "God, I am yours" is to say, "God, all I have is yours. My time is yours. My dreams are yours. My money is yours. My house is yours. My influence is yours. My collection of vintage Star Wars figurines and outdoor gear are mine (whoops, I slipped up there). I mean, yours. All. Is. Yours."

The Bible calls this stewardship. The moment we said "yes" to Jesus, we signed over the deed of everything we thought we owned. We are now temporary stewards or caretakers for the things God has chosen to place in our lives. I thought I understood this concept until one day God challenged my use of pronouns.

When our kids were very young, Sarah and I developed a Christmas tradition. We wanted to remind our family we are celebrating Christ's birth and not just loading piles of future trash under the tree. We found catalogs which allow people to buy a goat or chicken or mosquito nets for needy families in other parts of the world. One of these would be our gift to Jesus. We'd sit down and choose our gift; then we'd compile our family money (including the kids' allowance), put it all in an envelope with the picture of the goat (or whatever) on it, and place it under the tree.

I won't pretend; I was pretty proud of myself. It felt good inside. I thought, "God, isn't this wonderful? I'm using my money and giving it to your causes. I'm showing my kids what giving looks like." That self-satisfaction didn't last very long, however. I felt an inner gnaw. God was knocking on the door of my mind.

"Craig, whose money?"

"My money, God, for your work. Aren't you happy about that?" I whispered back.

"Craig, you said all you have is mine, right? You are the caretaker. I'm the king."

"Ooohhh," I started to realize. "It's your money, not mine? I'm returning back to you what is rightfully yours."

"Now you are getting it, Craig."

When the possessive pronoun changes from "mine" to "yours" it is a plate-tectonic level shift in our worldview. Who knew grammar could be so spiritual? Apparently, my seventh grade English teacher was on to something. We are kindly invited to return, not our resources, but his resources back to him: his time, his money, and so on. If we want to see multiplied miracles in our lives, step one is to understand who owns the resources. We have to drop the "my" and "mine" and replace it with "yours." Jesus communicated this concept through a parable (see Matthew 25:14–30) he once told about three managers who were given much in order to invest it wisely for the owner. Two of the managers did as the owner requested and were greatly rewarded; one manager did not follow through and suffered grave consequences. Similarly, when we see the things in our lives as God's, it positions us to be bold enough for step two.

Divine Math, Step 2: Release What's Already His

The second step to multiplied miracles through our lives is about release: releasing what's already his. The disciples had some bread and fish. They could have eaten the food, keeping it all to themselves.

If they consumed for themselves, that's all they would have had—partially satisfied bellies with starving crowds staring at them. If they kept what God had placed on loan into their hands, they would have never seen what God could do through them.

You and I have this same opportunity. We get salaries, we get twenty-four hours in a day, we have influence in certain circles. True, you need to eat. I need to eat. We need to wisely save for our kids' college education and our retirement. We want to have some fun hobbies on the side and go out to dinner and a movie now and then. Fine. But if that's all we do, that's all we'll have and that's all of God's power we will see: a home, food, education, a hobby here and there, retirement—then we die. But I think you want more out of your life than that. I know Christ wants more for you. No, I know he *has* more for you than that.

If we keep for ourselves, what we have is all we get. If we release back to God, we get to participate in multiplied miracles. When we keep for ourselves, there is a one-for-one return on our investment. When we release back to God, one plus one might equal one million, a multiplied miracle. If all you have is all you want, then cling to what is in your hands. If you long for more, get ready to release. You were made for God's work.

The release of our natural resources unleashes the power and potential of the supernatural. Remember our math equation?

Natural resources released + supernatural strength received = multiplied miracle

It's when we release back to God what is already rightfully his that he can take the natural and infuse it with the supernatural.

This makes me think of my friend Skip, who completed a prison sentence for a white-collar crime some years back. I know, not your average guy, but keep listening. He lost everything because of his mistakes. He did his time, paid back his debts, and then he needed a job. He worked hard, starting at minimum wage, and, over time, scraped together a little savings. You'd think a guy like that would be focused on rebuilding his own stockpile, maybe to get back on top to prove himself. But not Skip. He knew all he had was God's. He took the savings and rented a little space in an area where teenagers were on the streets ruining their lives. He started a simple after-school program. At first, he just had games, activities, and snacks for the youth—a hand-me-down foosball table, used board games, and day-old donated bagels from the shop down the road.

The students kept returning, volunteers kept showing up, and donations began pouring in. More resources came in and Skip kept releasing them back to God for God's work. Receive. Release. Receive. Release. Receive. Release. Then . . .

His ministry multiplied. He expanded from games to a Bible study to a full-blown youth program. He started providing professional counseling, job skills training, mentoring, support groups, and a donated clothing boutique for teen moms. This turned into a church for the forgotten youth on the side of town where no one ever wants to end up. There, students are finding faith in Christ, hope beyond the streets, help for tomorrow, and relationships with a small army of church volunteers who are investing in the lives of at-risk youth. Life isn't perfect, but Skip wakes up every single day with a paramount sense of purpose and unshakeable joy.

Why? Because Skip made a choice: he released the resources God placed in his hands. Sure, he had a little more perspective about what really matters after being in prison. But isn't his final destination the same as yours and mine? He was tangibly desperate. He could have used those "few loaves of bread and small fish" for himself, but his heart was devoted. He acknowledged he was on borrowed time. God was loaning him resources to be used for divine purposes. All was a gift and all belonged to God.

Had Skip decided to hang on to the starting minimum wage for himself, all he would have been supporting was his own struggle for survival. Instead, he had the guts to release back to God that which was already God's (his time and money). God multiplied it into so much more.

Here's the biblical truth about miracles. God will do the

supernatural. He will part the Red Sea, he will fill empty jars, he will feed thousands, he will lead people to faith in him, he will heal sickness, he will forgive sin, and so on. God will do the supernatural, but it often begins with the release of something we have. God asks his people first, "What do you have?" He invites his people to take the first step, to pour out the last drop, to give their own lives, to speak up, to step forward; then, he will change reality.

This is because he has designed us as his coworkers. "For we are co-workers in God's service . . ." (1 Corinthians 3:9).

You and I are invited to participate in God's plans. In fact, he desires our participation so much that he voluntarily resolves to do much of his work in the world through us rather than on his own. Our participation isn't just an afterthought to him; he allows us to be important to the work he is doing. When there is a project for God to do on this planet, he turns to you and me. Before God will bring his kingdom on earth as it is in heaven, he is looking for us to create a foothold by faith for it to take shape.

This is why Jesus doesn't just zap the hunger or make bread appear from nothing. He turns to the disciples and says, "What do you have?" He's inviting the disciples to be part of the solution, to join him in the work, and learn from him in the process. He's showing the disciples, he's showing us: "You are my hands and feet. You are the pathway for my power. You create a foothold by faith. You are the conduits of my kingdom. Release the resources in your hands, and you will be a part of my power multiplied into miracles from heaven."

Do you want this kind of impact from your life? I do! God has not placed you here just to receive from him and then struggle for your own survival or pleasure. Remember, you are blessed to be a blessing. You and I still have breath in our lungs because we are walking, talking conduits of his kingdom. We are here because there is work to be done and we are God's coworkers. When we cry out to God and say, "God, bring those people who are far from you into knowledge of your love and grace; God, feed the hungry; God, help the needy, God, stop sex-trafficking; God, build the church so it is thriving and so that young and old alike will find you" . . .—when we pray those kinds of prayers asking for God's miraculous intervention—his answer will likely be, "What do *you* have in *your* hands?" He'll be looking to us to release what's already his, so he can do what only he can do.

This is the opportunity you have with your one-and-only life; correction, with his one-and-only life which he's chosen to loan to you. Having the guts to release it is not easy, but the results are astounding.

A Word about Money

Let's talk specifically about money for a minute. We get funky when it comes to money. You may be ticked at TV evangelists who guilt-trip little old ladies to give while cruising around in private jets and taking staged pictures with malnourished babies; me too. To be clear, the resources we need to release go far beyond money. As I've mentioned, it's our time, education, position, influence, whatever. But we might as well tackle the tough one (money) first.

Why focus on talking about money? Because Jesus did. Sixteen of the thirty-eight parables Jesus told were about how to handle money and possessions. In the Gospels, a surprising one out of ten verses (288 in all) deal directly with the subject of money. The entire Bible offers five hundred verses on prayer, less than five hundred verses on faith, but more than two thousand verses on money and possessions.[1]

Some people misquote the Bible as saying, "Money is the root of all evil." What it *does* say is, "The *love* of money is the root of all kinds of evil" (1 Timothy 6:10 NLT, emphasis added). This is true whether you have money or you don't.

It's what you allow money to do in your heart which determines its power in your life. Will it grow into fertilizer for selfishness and greed within you? Will it fester fear in your soul and anxiety in your mind? Unchecked, it will accomplish all of that. Jesus says, "No one can serve two masters. . . . You cannot serve both God and money" (Matthew 6:24).

The only way, and I mean only way to get a grip on money's power in your heart, is to return it to its owner. And that's not you or me.

The Bible sets up a practice called tithing, which translates as "a tenth." We could define it as the "soul-sparing, insidious-effect-destroying act of returning money to God in order to see God's multiplied miracles." God's people are invited to return the first tenth of any income to their creator. Tithing is an investment, really. It's a choice to build God's enduring kingdom more than our own temporary castles.

When I first learned of this concept of tithing, it seemed impossible. I wanted to fix my car; I wanted to upgrade my dingy apartment; I wanted to get a new mountain bike; I knew I needed to start saving for the future. I couldn't do this. But then I found a surprising smack-down challenge from God—the only time in the Bible that we are told to test him:

> "Bring the whole tithe into the storehouse, that there may be food in my house. Test me in this," says the LORD Almighty, "and see if I will not throw open the floodgates of heaven and pour out so much blessing that there will not be room enough to store it."
>
> **—Malachi 3:10**

Why does God invite us to test him? Because he knows when we release the resources in our hands, he can multiply them into a miracle. The miracle isn't just for others either, it's for us as well! Sometimes the "so much blessing" comes back in a deep sense of joy or greater purpose to our jobs and lives. Sometimes it comes back with inner healing and great friendships. Sometimes (*not* always) the blessing returning to us is even financial. But it always comes back to us in freedom from the unrelenting grip of materialism.

I can't begin to write all the stories I have heard and experienced, stories of friends who decided to tithe for a starter period of ninety days and see what happened. What they thought would be a financial hit was returned to them with an unexpected raise or tax return or financial gift of an equal or greater amount than what they gave to God. Again, I'm not promising prosperity if you start tithing. Blessing may be financial, but it certainly shows up in many forms. You never know how God wants to pour back out to you.

When I started tithing, I couldn't do it. I trimmed back my monthly expenses to the wooden studs. I only had 2 percent which I could legitimately give while still feeding myself. So, I gave 2 percent. Then, I committed to raising the 2 percent to 10 percent, gradually over time. Tithing is now such a part of me, I'll never go back. I've been able to keep my heart serving God over money for more than twenty years. Sarah and I have invested in above-and-beyond efforts to grow the church, pull people out of cyclical poverty, sponsor orphans, and give to friends when prompted by the Holy Spirit. You name it. The joy we experience is unspeakable.

Imagine the sense of motivation you would receive from your job every day if getting money for yourself wasn't your only goal. Maybe you scale back the night out on the town and start giving to your church, knowing it will help to sponsor a night out for families with children with special needs. Imagine cranking on that spreadsheet or pushing through those sales calls with intense drive because more formatting and more calls equal more families cared for. That is a multiplied miracle!

By the way, this does not mean God wants you to live in poverty; it might mean he's okay with you going out to nice restaurants now and then.

[It is] good and fitting . . . to eat and drink and find enjoyment in all the toil with which one toils under the sun . . .

—Ecclesiastes 5:18

God wants you to enjoy life, the life he has given you. He wants you to be content.

Generally, the harder you work, the more fruits of your labor you get to enjoy. But the pleasures of this world are *nothing* compared to the multiplied miracles God wants to work in and through you because of the resources he's placed in your hands. Never settle for less. Never succumb to the love of money. Return back to God. Release what is his and you'll experience all he has for you.

A Warning about "When I, Then I" Thinking

One pitfall to pay attention to: I've found myself occasionally getting trapped in the "when I, then I" spiral. Maybe you can relate. *When* I have saved up enough for retirement, *then* I will be more generous. *When* I finish my exams, *then* I'll use my time to serve others. *When* I get a raise, *then* I will start tithing. The problem with "when I, then I" thinking is it never stops. There is always another desired threshold to cross, penny to save, or personal purchase to make. It also violates Jesus' vital principle of faithfulness, which he summarizes like this: "Whoever can be trusted with very little can also be trusted with much" (Luke 16:10).

If you're a boss, you don't give the big project to a new employee right away. You give them small tasks first, see how they handle those small tasks, and then entrust them with larger tasks. It's the same with God and the resources he places into our lives for his purposes. He invites us to be faithful with what's already in our hands. He wants us to develop muscles of faithfulness, generosity, and a his-versus-mine mentality in small ways. Out of love and understanding, God wants us to grow the skill of release before he grows what we receive. Start releasing right away. Don't wait. We might not have tomorrow; we only have today to be faithful.

The world screams a different message. While you are reading this, people are getting paid millions, possibly billions of dollars to figure out how to convince you and me to consume more, to horde more, to get more for ourselves. We exist in a never-ending barrage of self-focused indulgence. Never forget, what you keep for yourself is all you get. What you release back to God will be multiplied into his miracles in your life and in this world.

I've had the weighty privilege of sitting by the bedside of people who were passing away. I've walked families through the process of pulling life support from their loved ones. Never once has anyone said, "I wish I had accumulated more for myself. I wish I had focused more on my own needs." Rather, I've celebrated with people who have built churches, fought poverty, served others, and left a legacy of human generosity, the investments they made while they still could have left a lasting imprint of God's multiplied miracles on this world. "What good is it for someone to gain the whole world, yet forfeit their soul?" (Mark 8:36).

You are God's coworker. You create a foothold for his kingdom. He has loaned you resources to release for others to receive from him; if you do, you will experience more multiplied miracles than you can imagine. This is the life you were made to live.

CHAPTER 10

A Surprising Blessing

Have you ever sensed that you are missing out on some of what God has for you, as if there is a barrier to God's blessing in your life? I have, and as a result, I felt farther away from God's presence.

If you haven't experienced this confusing distance yet, you will. But you aren't alone. Even after trusting in Jesus, many Christians live with a valuable, unused "gift card" forgotten in the dresser drawers of life. Through Jesus, all of God's blessing and presence is already credited to us, but because of these barriers to blessing we leave something untapped and remain underdeveloped. We live with a gnawing sense that we aren't seeing all of God or experiencing all of who he is, that we're missing some of what he wants to accomplish in and through our lives.

It doesn't need to remain this way though. We can remove the barriers and reclaim what we might be missing—a surprising blessing.

I once overcame a significant barrier and rediscovered blessing in the middle of the desert—not a figurative, spiritual-metaphor desert; I mean an actual desert. I'll explain.

This was a busy season of life. Sarah and I worked all day and into most evenings. We were handling different challenging situations in our jobs, our kids were adjusting to school, our extended families were facing health issues, we had a new puppy who liked to pee on the carpet, our closets and garage were still full of boxes daily reminding us, "You still have so much undone in the corners of your life."

I had been a Christian for some time, so I knew that my walk with God would have its ups and downs. I knew he was with me and that I was not hiding anything from him. Still, the words of Scripture weren't grabbing my attention. My prayers were dusty. My heart and energy toward him felt flighty. My faith droned on in monotone. Something wasn't as it was meant to be.

We decided to join a group from our church to go on a service trip to Mexico. We drove to Juárez, Mexico, on a school break to build a home for a single mother, Ana. She had escaped from years of being physically abused and was now trying to raise four children on her own. With the financial help of her local church in Juárez and the sweat equity from her and other members of the congregation, we were there to provide a little boost toward finishing the project.

A quick side note: Mission trips like these can be tricky; much research has been done and many volumes written on whether they are helping or hurting a local situation. One of the challenges is that volunteers get swept into a colonial-esque, savior complex. "We're here to help pull you out of poverty with our strength, money, and know-how." Then they disappear. This attitude of drive-by superiority is damaging. However, despite the many potential pitfalls of mission trips and similar serving experiences, I believe if we listen, learn, and adjust over time, we can avoid many of the destructive consequences. Done with humility and care, these relationships can lead to mutual development and shared goals.

I had scheduled this trip some months prior, mostly because I was working in a church, the missions department reported to me, and I needed to check in on some of our partner ministries. I'm not proud of the uninspired motivation here . . . not a great start. But I was tired at the time, so I assumed what I needed to recharge my soul was a week on the beach lounging in Cancún or San Diego. Juárez isn't exactly known for the decadent relaxation I was seeking.

God knew I needed a different type of recalibration.

We worked hard and built the home. The moment that we handed the keys of the completed house to Ana and her children shook me. We formed a little circle around them just outside the cinder block doorway. We asked Ana if we could pray for her. She said "Yes, thank you, but first may I please pray for all of you?" I wasn't expecting this from Ana.

She started speaking in Spanish (with the help of a translator), "God, you are so good and so loving. Bless each person and each family here. Fill their lives and hearts with your presence; let them see how close you are; help them with their needs. Right now, Lord, let them see you and your great love." On and on she prayed like this.

This may sound strange to you, but it is what it is. During Ana's prayer I felt the literal rush of the Holy Spirit in ways I don't remember ever happening before in my life. It was an inner electricity that grabbed me. I was filled with the warmth of God, an unexplainable sensation of concentrated joy and peace and closeness with him. My eyes filled up with tears. I felt God's power and all I wanted to do was pray and sing and thank him. Worries and cares faded into nothing. I had crystal-clear awareness of the God of heaven. Wow! Where had that been in the middle of my dry faith?

I quickly reflected: a struggling, homeless, abused, single mother in the scarred desert backroads of Juárez, Mexico, prayed over me the most unexpected, powerful prayer I could ever remember. Through this beautiful but very broken and forgotten woman, I experienced God bursting into my life in an unexpected way. As she prayed, I had this acute sense that Jesus himself was praying for me. This was a surprise blessing.

A flood of Scripture started reminding me of some essential truths that Christians, especially in more privileged circumstances, often forget. "For he [God] stands at the right hand of the needy . . ." (Psalm 109:31).

As Christians we may have a few bad days and then we pray, "God, I don't sense your presence in my life, you feel far away. God, where are you? Why don't you seem close?"

"I'm right here," God essentially says, according to the psalmist, "I'm right next to the people in need. Where are you?"

Jesus confirms what the psalmist is describing here. Jesus once was asked how he can be found. Paraphrasing his answer from Matthew 25, Jesus says:

> "You'll find me and experience me when you are with those who are hungry and thirsty and without shelter. You'll see me through those who are sick and in need and even those who are in prison without hope for a future. If you want to be with me, be with them. You'll find me among people in poverty, among those who are hurting and trapped. You'll experience me when you serve them."

My paraphrase: If you want to increase your awareness of God's presence in your life, increase your proximity to the poor.

The promises from the prophet Isaiah in the Old Testament go even further:

> . . . if you spend yourselves in behalf of the hungry
>   and satisfy the needs of the oppressed,
> then your light will rise in the darkness,
>   and your night will become like the noonday.
>
> **—Isaiah 58:10**

My summary: serve those in poverty and the oppressed and you will shine brighter than all those around you. The more you give to those in need, the more God's blessing will shine through your life. Listen to what Isaiah says next. As a result of "spend[ing] yourselves in behalf of the hungry and satisfy[ing] the needs of the oppressed . . ."

> The LORD will guide you always;
>   he will satisfy your needs in a sun-scorched land

and will strengthen your frame.
You will be like a well-watered garden,
like a spring whose waters never fail.

—Isaiah 58:11

Give to Get. Yep.

You might be thinking right about now, "Craig, this chapter is a little backward. Shouldn't we want to serve the poor because it is the right thing to do? You are saying we should serve the poor because we get something more from God out of helping others?"

Yep. Serve people in need and you will be blessed (*and* because it is absolutely the right thing to do). That's exactly what I am saying. Not because I want to twist the motivations of your heart. I'm saying it because God said it. He didn't even shy away from motivating us to care by promising us more in return. He's very clear throughout Scripture that the more we give, the more we receive. We reap what we sow. We see this in Isaiah 58. When you spend yourself on behalf of those in need, the Lord promises to:

". . . guide you always, he will satisfy your needs in the sun-scorched land and will strengthen your frame. You will be like a well-watered garden, like a spring whose waters never fail."

Wow!

Through serving and caring for those oppressed and in need, you'll flourish, God says, in physical, spiritual, and relational ways. You'll be under the cover of God's blessing in every area of your life, like a garden that gets just the right amount of rain.

The blessings you receive as you care for those in need may not be a full bank account, zero problems in life, and perfect relationships. But when I've served others, especially those in great need, I've been blessed in the process. Sometimes it's through seeing in them a level of contentment with the little they have that convicts and inspires me to free myself from material addiction and pettiness. Sometimes it's through the exuberant gratitude, joy, and faith they radiate, as when Ana prayed for me. Other times my faith matures just by sharing in the pain of another when there are no easy answers or easy ways out.

I think about a man named John, on death row in the Louisiana state penitentiary, whom I counseled and prayed with once. He was fully repentant and brokenhearted for the crime he had committed many years prior. He had asked Jesus and the family he'd grieved for forgiveness, but he knew he still had to pay the earthly price for his crime with his life. He knew that Jesus died in his place on the cross, so he could be made right with the Father in heaven. John gave me a cross he stitched together out of yarn to remind me of the power of Jesus' death. It was a more meaningful reflection on the cross of Christ than I've ever had; what a surprise blessing!

I remember the man whom I met with who was being evicted because he lost his job due to chronic injuries and couldn't pay his bills. I had helped him through some tough situations in his marriage and he wanted to thank me. He knew I was from Chicago and loved the Bulls. Although he had very little, he thanked me by giving me his collector's Scottie Pippen championship basketball card for my son. I tried not to accept it, but he refused and wanted the chance to give what he had. Amazing generosity.

I remember countless meals made with joy and sacrifice by people who could hardly afford enough food for themselves. One family could only purchase meat once a month. I was invited into their home for dinner after helping out in their community. While we sat together on their dirt floor, what do you think they served me? Their monthly ration of goat meat. Just for me. I'm not exactly a goat meat connoisseur, but I do want to live with radical generosity like they do. Other meals with similarly generous families, including boiled carp, chicken feet, yak milk curds, and powdered eggs didn't exactly hit the spot. But the freshly made banana bread, mangos, fried chicken, home-ground tortillas, and beans sure did! With every one of those meals I received from people with very little material wealth, I was reminded of the overwhelming provision of God, filled with gratitude, and challenged to live a more generous life myself.

I've never been around worship that was so vibrant and worshiped with such unmistakable and pure dependence on God than with those who lived on one meal or less per day.

I've never been around people who are as sensitive to the Holy Spirit's whispers and cling to Christ with healthy, biblical desperation than those who don't know how they will be able to provide for the basic needs of their children.

I've never seen people with as much peace when the chaos of circumstances surrounds them than when I am with those whose limiting life challenges would crush many others.

We All Struggle. We All Have Need. We All Live in Poverty.

I'm not attempting to aggrandize poverty. Some of you reading this right now are experiencing the pain poverty brings. It is brutal. And, certainly, those struggling with poverty do not always reflect the qualities I've mentioned. However, when we are in need, we have a greater opportunity to learn to rely on Jesus and build more spiritual muscle in the process. Poverty—whether physical, or emotional, or relational—is the training ground for developing dependence and gratitude. When we cry out to Jesus, he meets us in our poverty. Do we all always take advantage of that opportunity? No. But many do, and we can learn from them.

We can learn from the dependency they have on Jesus to bring our own (possibly less obvious) needs to God in faith as well. We can learn to surrender our anxiety and discontentment while sitting alongside the hospital bed of someone terminally ill. We can let go of the death grip of greed and materialism when we look into the eyes and lives of those living in other socioeconomic situations than our own.

What we discover when we embrace others in poverty is that we all have a type of poverty; a poverty of the soul. When we face this vulnerably, then Christ in us can begin to commune with Christ in others. Take a look at this sage insight from the great Henri Nouwen:

> When we are not afraid to confess our own poverty, we will be able to be with other people in theirs. The Christ who lives in our own poverty recognizes the Christ who lives in other people's. Just as we are inclined to ignore our own poverty, we are inclined to ignore others'. We prefer not to see people as destitute; we do not like to look at people who are deformed or disabled, we avoid talking about people's pain and sorrows, we stay away from brokenness, helplessness, and neediness.
>
> By this avoidance, we might lose touch with the people through whom God is manifested in us. But when we have discovered God in our own poverty, we will lose our fear of the poor and go to them and meet God.[1]

We cannot miss these surprise blessings. I'll let Scripture drive home this point:

> Give generously to them and do so without a grudging heart; then because of this the LORD your God will bless you in all your work and in everything you put your hand to.
>
> **—Deuteronomy 15:10**

> The generous will themselves be blessed, for they share their food with the poor.
>
> **—Proverbs 22:9**

> Whoever is kind to the poor lends to the LORD, and he will reward them for what they have done.
>
> **—Proverbs 19:17**

Do not neglect to do good and to share what you have, for such sacrifices are pleasing to God.

—Hebrews 13:16 ESV

"Give, and it will be given to you. Good measure, pressed down, shaken together, running over, will be put into your lap. For with the measure you use it will be measured back to you."

—Luke 6:38 ESV

Those who give to the poor will lack nothing, but those who close their eyes to them receive many curses.

—Proverbs 28:27

If you ever find yourself in a season of monotonous faith, dry prayers, and a sense of distance from God, examine your life. Are you as near to, involved with, and sacrificially generous toward those in need as the Lord has spelled out in Scripture? His commands and promises are clear on this one.

If you want to increase your awareness of God's presence in your life, increase your proximity to the poor. If you want God's blessings to flow into your life, let tangible love, care, and concern for those in need pour out of your life. If you and I are not personally serving people in poverty, then you and I are missing out on massive amounts of God's presence and blessing for ourselves.

How Do We Do This?

So how do you build this practice of proximity and service to those in need into your life? First, don't make it more complicated than it needs to be. You may remember the old Nike commercials "Just do it" (am I dating myself again?); it's kind of like that. You just have to do it. Give generously. Reorient some of your time to invest in others. At the end of a week or a month, ask yourself, "Where have

I used my time, money, aspirations, and energy for someone in need other than myself and my own immediate family?"

It's possible you are in a season of life where your own challenges are screaming in your ears; your own needs are scrambling for everything you've got. If you are in absolute crisis survival mode then, like a tree in winter, you probably feel like you need to focus your energy inward to strengthen your own root system. God does sometimes call us to take care of our own house first. But Jesus also praises a widow who gives all she has out of her poverty (see Luke 21:1–4). So, here's the thing: don't let your inward focus last for too long. Springtime always emerges. You'll miss out on a blessing for yourself and you'll miss seeing God work through you to help another.

A Side Note for Readers of Privilege

If you look around and find yourself surrounded by a suburban daydream or privileged circumstances, have more than you know you need, or realize the people you spend time with seem put together and perfect, I have two thoughts for you to consider.

First, there *are* needs all around you. Likely your neighbors are struggling in some way, your coworkers could use your heartfelt attention, or an old friend might be in a financial fix. Ask God to help you see as he sees. He will open your eyes to the needs around you and invite you by his Holy Spirit to appropriately and maybe sacrificially meet those needs.

Second, you may have to be intentional and choose to get out of the bubble you are dangerously stuck within. Writing checks is one thing, and it is helpful and needed. But if you stay at check-writing distance you miss the transformational relationships found only in proximity to those in need and the presence of God in that space. You may need to sign up for a volunteer team at church or at a shelter a few communities away. You may need to take a risk and participate on a short-term project. You may need to give youth mentoring or elderly visitation a try. If you don't regularly encounter people in need in your daily life, you will have to change how you live to align your life with the heart of Jesus.

For those of you who are parents, please give this gift to your children and let them quickly learn to be generous and take risks to care for those in need. This is the heart God wants to shape in them.

A Caution for All of Us

One freeing caution for you. Not all needs are yours to bear. It can feel impossible to walk through a street passing one homeless person after another. Or seeing opportunities to help others pile up. I've experienced that guilty conscience which sets in and says, "Craig, you won't be a good Christian if you don't feed all of those people and help them get a home and job." Or, "Craig how can you even go on a vacation when you could be on a service trip instead?"

The critical question is this: "God, what is mine to do?" You and I don't have enough money or time to solve all the problems we see or needs we come across. Also, it's important to take care of yourself and your family. You can be released from any guilt just by asking God to lead you.

Remember, you are filled with the Holy Spirit. There will be times where he tells you, "Yes, go for it; give that person everything in your wallet or sign up for that volunteering rotation on Monday nights." Say "yes" to mentoring that at-risk sixteen-year-old this year or going on that mission trip. But there will also be times when he says, "That's not yours to do."

Sometimes it can be difficult to determine whether God's Spirit is really releasing us from something, or whether our own hearts just don't want to do it. Here is when we need to practice discernment with an open heart. Stay with the question for a while. Search your heart to become aware of any of your own hindrances or objections. Bring those into the light through prayer and then listen intently to the Spirit. This takes time and practice. Follow his lead and say "no" to any voice of guilt or condemnation that tries to drag you down.

A Story of Hidden Need

Over the past couple of years our church community in the suburbs of Denver has taken enormous steps to grow at serving those in need. We are planted in the center of a suburban bubble and wrongly thought, "The needs around us aren't too prevalent." But we decided to meet with our county leaders and ask them, "How can we help? What are the greatest needs in the community?" To our surprise, they said that suburban homelessness was one of their greatest challenges to solve. "Right now, in our community we know of nine hundred homeless students who are registered in the school system. Most of the families are single-parent, working at least one job, if not more, and are still in poverty. They live out of cars, motels, sleep on other people's couches—you name it. And there are no shelters or transitional housing programs in our community to help these families transition out of poverty. Can your church help?"

Nine hundred children without a home in our little suburban bubble neighborhood! We started praying as a church. We studied Scripture and decided, "This is not right. We are told to love our neighbor, and our neighbor doesn't have a home." We resolved, "We will work together with the county officials and other church communities in our area to completely end homelessness in our county. That's right; we'll stop when every single child and their family has a home and is lifted out of poverty."

This is no easy task. We brought in experts, studied different programs, and ultimately launched a multifaceted effort to meet the immediate needs of food, clothing, and shelter for these families, while at the same time equipping them over the long-term with training and mentoring for life skills, job skills, and spiritual renewal.

The response has been overwhelming. People in our congregation who drove to and from work and never set foot out of their garage have signed up to serve meals and provide clothing and shelter for single moms and their children. A group of volunteers called "allies" meets every week in a mentoring and friendship-building relationship with one of these precious families transitioning out of poverty. The allies, along with single mothers, attend classes together, and process what they learn to figure out how to apply it to life. To help out, people in the church are now donating cars and homes on a temporary basis. We've even had some business owners rally together to free up fifty apartments (set aside for corporate housing) for families in this program.

Imagine how everyone is impacted. The church families have an intense sense of purpose and God's blessing in their lives. They've literally discovered more of Christ in the relationships they've formed with those in need. The recipient families have an answer to prayer and an enormous pressure released so they can work to change their situation. Hope in some cases has been restored for those who have lost all hope. And the watching community has been inspired to live with greater levels of generosity.

This is an incredible adventure which we get to be a part of. Serving others transforms our lives, changes the lives of those whom we help, and shines a little more of heaven into our broken world.

It's worth repeating one final time as we close this chapter: If you want to increase your awareness of God's presence in your life, increase your proximity to the poor. If you want God's blessings to flow into your life, let tangible love, care, and concern for those in need pour out of your life.

CHAPTER 11

A Surprising Mission

I'd never seen Tom before. He stopped me in the church hallway one random afternoon and asked if we could talk. He knew I was a pastor.

"I've never come to your church. I'm sorry about that, but I have an important question for you. If God is real, do you think he loves people who take their own life?"

Whoa. Whatever you answer next in a conversation like this determines some serious outcomes.

"Tom, I'm so glad you found me. Let's sit down and talk. Where is that question coming from? I'd love to hear what is on your mind." Then I used the three most important words I've ever learned for difficult conversations: "Tell me more."

Tom continued to share his situation. He was a drummer for a well-known heavy-metal hair band in the '80s. He even showed me a picture from the glory days. He'd gotten caught up in the whirlwind of sex, drugs, and rock 'n' roll and ended up distant from everyone who loved him. Most of his family had stopped talking with him. He was on his own now and had been diagnosed with stage IV tongue cancer. The doctors said he had only months to live. Treatment would likely be brutal, leaving little chance of a true recovery. He'd already had all his teeth pulled, but he'd need to have his tongue completely removed and would likely have to live off a feeding tube. He wanted to end the suffering, but he also wanted peace with God.

The idea of a suffering death caving in on me as it was on Tom caused me to question if *I'd* have the strength to naturally endure. But I asked Tom, "Would you please give God a chance to help you? If you take your own life, then it's over. But what if there is more? What if God is real and has more for you? Give him a chance; let's walk this journey." I wanted Tom to receive a gift he'd never thought possible.

We'll come back to Tom later. For now, let's shift gears and talk about gifts for a moment.

The Greatest Gift

What's the best present you've ever received? Don't worry, you don't have to pretend to be spiritual here.

I know mine. I was ten years old. It was the morning of my birthday; my parents woke me up and brought me downstairs for breakfast. I'm thinking, "Oh, yeah, bring it on! Birthday present time!"

Except, major letdown, they just brought me downstairs for breakfast; that's it.

I downed those Corn Pops like I hadn't eaten in a week, thinking gift time would come quickly. But still no present. They had me call my grandma and grandpa (Nana and Bopa) and open cards from my extended family. It was all nice, but still no present. This was a tough waiting game; did they think I was some sort of patience ninja?

Then they said, "Craig, will you go into the living room and grab the newspaper, please?"

"Sure," I said, wondering if this might be a diversion.

But what I found instead was an old blanket covering something enormous. I whipped the blanket to the side and there it was: a shiny, perfectly assembled, yellow-and-black Huffy BMX bike.

"Yesss!" I screamed out loud. "Thank you!"

I jumped on the bike and didn't bother to take it outside first. I rode it straight out of the living room, popping a wheelie in the hallway. I jumped off just enough to open the front door, and then I tore down to trails and jumps that weren't too far away from my house. Ahhh, to be ten years old on a BMX bike in the middle of summer again!

There is nothing like receiving *that* gift—the gift you've been building toward, hoping for, desperately needing. Or at least desperately wanting. It's hard to compare the sensation.

The only thing that compares is the feeling my parents had giving me that bike. I know what that feeling is like now that I have my own kids. I know what easily beats the feeling of opening your most desired gift; it's giving someone else their most desired gift. The wattage of fulfillment you receive when giving someone a gift they have yearned for far outweighs getting your own gift. Like when Sarah and I gave our daughter the dollhouse she was hoping for; her face lit up so beautifully when she first saw it. Or when I surprised my son and pulled him out of school to go skiing together on a powder day. (Some things are just more important than school!) Or when I get to take the kids all weekend, so Sarah can get away with friends or by herself to recharge. That is exciting. Honestly, it's stupid fun.

There is no greater joy than giving a good gift. Yet our gift-giving excitement is a small reflection of how God feels when he gives the gift of abundant life. His gift is the gift of grace, given through his perfect Son Jesus Christ. Though the verse may be often used, John 3:16 is rich with meaning and perfect theology (beliefs about the nature of God):

> "For God so loved the world that he gave his one and only Son, that whoever believes in him shall not perish but have eternal life."
>
> **—John 3:16**

God's love through Jesus Christ is the greatest gift anyone truly can receive. (It's time to get spiritual now, though BMX bikes are still very important in the scheme of things.) And God loves to give away his love! According to John 10:10, Jesus says, "I have come that they may have life, and have it to the full."

God longs for people to have complete life-to-the-brim unconditional love and total forgiveness. He spares nothing. He wants to give the gift of salvation through Jesus to all people. He gave that gift to you and me and it transformed our lives.

But, and this is critical, he doesn't just give you and me a gift for us to keep for ourselves. He immediately enlists us as part of his crew. The moment we receive the gift of grace we are commissioned to be on his gift-giving team.

Jesus once compared the kingdom of God and our involvement as his followers to a feast (see Luke 14:16–23). He said, "A certain man was preparing a great banquet and invited many guests" (verse 16).

Picture a Mediterranean party thrown by a wealthy king. Spiced meats and creamy sauces, steaming rice and fresh baked breads, colorful fruits and piles of vegetables, jugs of wine and pitchers of ale, fine linen draped everywhere, live musicians spread throughout the room, a lengthwise table as far as you can see.

At the time of the banquet he sent his servant to tell those who had been invited, "Come, for everything is now ready."

But they all alike began to make excuses . . .

—Luke 14:17–18

Fast forwarding.

The servant came back and reported this to his master. Then the owner of the house became angry and ordered his servant, "Go out quickly into the streets and alleys of the town and bring in the poor, the crippled, the blind and the lame."

"Sir," the servant said, "what you ordered has been done, but there is still room."

Then the master told his servant, "Go out to the roads

and country lanes and compel them to come in, so that my house will be full."

—Luke 14:21–23

"My desire," God says, "is that everyone will be with me at my banquet. I want this place full!" When you and I became followers of Jesus, we were given a seat at the table with him. We were invited to the feast: all of his love, all of his presence, all of his power, all of his purpose, all of his forgiveness. It's all right here for you and me—given to us because of Jesus' death and resurrection and through the presence of the Holy Spirit in our lives. When we enjoy all of God in this way, it brings him glory (to use a biblical term) and gives us pure delight.

But have you ever wondered, as I have, "God what is my purpose now, really? Just to be close to you and wait until I die and go to heaven? What am I supposed to accomplish while I'm still alive?"

This great banquet picture and second Peter 3:9 (below) give us the answer to the reason you and I still breathe and the explanation for why Jesus hasn't returned to bring all time to completion.

. . . he is patient with you, not wanting anyone to perish, but everyone to come to repentance.

God is holding out on all of heaven; he is keeping you and me here on earth right now in order to invite others to the feast. He's delaying so that more invitations can go out, so that more can know him, more can experience him . . . and he's tapped you and me to be the invitation givers.

There is no greater gift you can give someone than an introduction to the God who loves them. There is no better use of your one and only life than to invite others to receive God's love. Period. We live to make invitations to the table of God's grace.

I love inviting people to parties. Who wouldn't, right? It's all about connecting and creating space for relationships to flourish, having a good time, and enjoying an evening. Unfortunately, when it comes to inviting people into a relationship with God (evangelism), many Christians over the years have turned people away with how they've made the invitation. As Gandhi once reportedly stated after trying to enter a church to find out about Jesus and being turned away, "If it weren't for Christians, I'd be a Christian."

I realize you might be thinking, "Wait a minute, Craig. Did you just trick this chapter into being about evangelism? That's a dirty word. No way! I'm not going to become one of those TV preachers full of hypocrisy or a Bible thrower on college campuses reminding everyone they will burn in hell. I'm not going to knock on random strangers' doors and shove cheaply printed literature in their face to tell them to stop sinning. Don't even go there, Craig."

I'll admit, one of the reasons I was extremely hesitant to become a Christian is because I didn't want to be like *that*. I didn't want to be one of those pushy weirdos, and I know you don't either. So, I won't go there. If you *do* want to become a pushy weirdo, it's easy. Just get really angry at other people for not following Jesus, begin to think you're superior to them because you now know the truth, and focus on telling them all the ways they are wrong and you are right. That's how we can not only push people away from us but also away from the God who loves them.

Most Christ-followers understandably abhor these pushy ideas of evangelism. So, they decide to quietly hold back and just "let their life speak." There is some wisdom in this: live with integrity, compel people with your heart, your choices, and the fruit of your life. But this is surprisingly not the most loving approach. The most loving thing we can do is share the greatest gift we can with others, not to hold out on them. At some point we must *tell* people how Jesus has transformed our lives and can revolutionize theirs. God gave us words and we must use them. Jesus' final words give us some direction about this:

"Go, and make disciples of all nations, baptizing them in the name of the Father and of the Son and of the Holy Spirit."

—Matthew 28:19

You can't fulfill the words of Jesus without using the words he's given you. Don't abdicate evangelism. Just find a way to do it well. You can take on this mission of inviting others into a relationship with God without becoming a pushy weirdo. Jesus even said in the parable we just studied, "*Compel* them to come in!"

We can evangelize in a compelling way! That was Jesus' vision. May I give you some advice on what loving, compelling, and effective evangelism can look like from Jesus' picture of the banquet? There are a few keys to remember and some behaviors to avoid.

Invite Them to the Party

First of all, our task is to invite people to a party. Remember, we are giving out party invitations, not telling non-Christians how their lives are wrong. When you invite someone to a party, you focus on how good the party is and the bigheartedness of the host. You might describe some of the food and music in detail. You might tell them how much you enjoyed the party the same host threw in the past. You might tell them how much the host wants them to be there.

Some have turned evangelism into pointing out all the wrong things in someone's life. "You are bad, you are broken, you are sinning, you are empty, you are going to hell . . ." Fill in the blank. This is not extending an invitation to an incredible party. This is an angry teacher handing out failure notices, and that's not what we've been asked to do!

Let me pull out of the analogy for a moment. Just tell people how much God loves them. Tell them how you felt when you were invited to be with him. Tell them the difference Jesus made in your life. Tell them how much joy and love and peace and power and purpose you are discovering in a relationship with Jesus. The point is the party. Our job is to invite people there.

As for telling people to stop sinning, that instruction is meant for fellow "believers" (brothers or sisters in the faith) who are close to us, and to point out their sin privately to them. The apostle Paul says explicitly that we should "restore [them] gently" (Galatians 6:1).

173

However, when it comes to "non-believers," Jesus is very clear who does the judging.

> "When he [the Holy Spirit] comes, he will prove the world to be in the wrong about sin and righteousness and judgment . . ."
>
> **—John 16:8**

And Paul adds:

> For what have I to do with judging outsiders? Is it not those inside the church whom you are to judge? God judges those outside . . .
>
> **—1 Corinthians 5:12–13 ESV**

Whose job is it to point out sin to the world? Is it the Christian's job? Nope! The Holy Spirit will manage that task. It's not a good idea to take over a role God has said is his alone. God will handle the sin awareness and judgment stuff for those outside of the faith, and he will do that graciously and gradually. When it comes to sharing with those who don't know Christ, you and I are supposed to handle the party invitations. Let's focus on sharing the complete transformation God can bring. Let's stay in our lane and keep judgment out of it.

Ineffective Christian evangelism has often followed this pattern: change your behaviors first; then, change your beliefs; and, finally, you will belong. Unfortunately, this is quite the opposite from my understanding of Scripture.

We are first called to invite people to belong, to see they can become adopted children of God. Belonging is disarming and opens their hearts to want to change their beliefs. They begin to see "maybe there is hope and purpose and truth and love beyond what I've known." They begin to believe God is real and his love and forgiveness are available to them. Then, when they choose to trust in Christ, which includes a confession of sin, they are filled with the Spirit, and the Spirit does an inside job. The Spirit leads people into new behaviors, inspired out of gratitude and conviction of the love of their Lord.

We do want to show people a vision for right living, of course. And part of this includes communicating the reality that we all fall short of the goodness, righteousness, and fulfillment God longs for us to have. Yet, because God welcomes people into the feast, our first priority is to help people belong to the community. If we mix this up, we may be damaging the hearts and souls whom Jesus died for.

Don't Do All the Talking

Another unintentionally damaging evangelism mix-up Christians often make is not being able to stop talking. You've been there at the barbecue where you meet someone who won't stop sharing what they know and what they think. It's a verbal narcissism grenade.

Christians can develop painful anxiety and sweaty palms when it comes to evangelism. They feel they are supposed to tell people the good news about Jesus and feel guilty when they haven't. So, in an edgy way at a socially uncomfortable moment, they often work up the courage to finally blurt something out about Jesus and the death penalty and the blood of the lamb and putting up a white flag of surrender and eternity with angels in heaven. They quote a bunch of Scripture and may draw a picture on a napkin. After a long monologue, they finally ask, "Are you ready to totally devote your life to Jesus now?" Phew. There was hardly time to breathe.

There was one important ingredient missing. Listening.

Have you ever noticed this verse in Ecclesiastes 3:11?

He has made everything beautiful in its time. He has also set eternity in the human heart . . .

If you want to be effective at sharing God's love with others, you must start from this core perspective; God is already at work within the people whom we are inviting to him. The message of hope and the desire for Jesus is already planted as a seed in their hearts. When God designed all people, he placed eternity in their hearts. Our job is not to jam a foreign concept into people's minds or to manipulate them toward our desired outcome. Rather, we are to draw out the longing for the Lord and the work of God that is already happening in their lives. The only way we can do that is by asking questions and by listening to them.

This is one of the reasons I love Alpha, the nonprofit organization I work for, and the way that Alpha equips churches in evangelism. It's quite simple, really, and it's based on listening. It's a gathering of as few as five to nine people or 500–900 people in multiple groups. There's a tasty meal (sounds like a banquet already). There's a short talk or great Alpha film. It's always high-quality, to the point, and brimming with grace, truth, and thoughtfulness. Then, the remaining hour is discussion. Open, safe, hospitable discussion. But the key is there are just a couple of well-trained Christians in the group who only ask questions. The rest of the group consists of people with doubts, questions, or even hostility to the faith. We say, "The film is our chance to share a bit about what we think as Christians, but the next hour is for you to share what you think—both to ask your questions and share your point of view. We won't correct you, we won't judge you, and we won't tell you to think differently. We'll just listen!"

The trained Christian hosts facilitate the conversation, saying things such as, "Tell me more. How did you come to think that? What other thoughts or experiences do you have which might shape that point of view?" Rather than wielding a hammer of God's truth to smack into other people, Christians are trained to view the process more as a loving exploration together. In asking questions of those who are seeking, it allows them to discover the eternity God has already placed in their hearts. It allows them to find the seeds of God's kingdom which have already been planted in them.

Author and theologian David Augsburger says, "Being heard is so close to being loved that for the average person they are almost indistinguishable."[1] Letting people share their thoughts over a meal and genuinely listening to them is loving them. Love which consists of such listening breaks down walls and opens people's hearts to want to know more.

Many people who are holding back from trusting Jesus are doing so not because of an intellectual question, but rather from a wounded or fearful heart (pride and rebellion are often just covering up wounds and fear). They may present intellectual issues like, "How can you prove God exists? Why would a good God allow suffering in this world? Is Jesus really who he said he was?" But the primary issue is a heart issue, not a head issue.

When people have inner hurts, instead of jumping in with a quick answer (if there is one), I ask follow-up questions about their lives. I discovered one person lost her mother when she was seven. Another person's brother died in a car wreck when he was seventeen. Now we are at a place where God can meet them. Yes, they will need some breakthrough in understanding at some point, but what they need first is an experience of listening through God's people.

Let God Do the Work

Finally, we must not become confused about what really changes someone's heart. If we think the power comes from our own well-timed or well-prepared answers to people's questions, then we will focus on providing answers. If we think the power comes from the energy we put into refuting bad beliefs about faith and wrong ideas of God, then we will put up a fight. But if we think the power comes from more than our explanations, we will do something different.

We must remember Romans 1:16: ". . . [the gospel] is the power of God that brings salvation to everyone who believes . . ."

The power is not in the arguments or the strategy or the evangelistic explanations to bring salvation. It's the power of God breaking into someone's heart which brings them to new life in Jesus.

We must be able to move beyond cerebral explanations about God and shift into guiding people into a heartfelt experience with

God. Ultimately, people are not longing for a new religion; they are yearning for a relationship with their Creator who loves them. Answers to questions are very helpful, but at some point explanations fail, and then you must invite people to just begin experiencing God for themselves. You can do this by praying for people on your own. You can ask people if you can pray for them. And you can, at the right time, invite people to pray themselves or with you.

God loves them, and God will show up for them.

It makes me think of Brian, a police officer who experienced many deadly and destructive tragedies. He said, "My heart grew a concrete wall around it; I was shut down." He came to Alpha meetings to explore faith and for weeks said, "God is not real—not when the suffering I've seen still happens." No explanation could change his heart. No human effort could rewire his soul. One evening, Brian attempted to pray for the first time (even though he didn't believe in God). "Come, Holy Spirit," he said and then waited. Within minutes, he was weeping and praying with his group: "I have no idea what happened, but I literally felt the concrete wall around my heart shatter and love pour in. And now, all I know is I *love* Jesus!" Brian asked Jesus for forgiveness and for his leadership. Brian acknowledged Jesus' death and resurrection and was baptized weeks later. Listening, belonging, friendship, and prayer over time opened up Brian's heart, and God did what only he can do: bring salvation.

Brian was invited to the party. He had a great meal with people who showed him he belonged. People listened to him, and over the course of time the longings inside his heart emerged. He was invited into an experience of God, not just an explanation about God—and it changed him forever.

Brian is now inviting others. He was baptized with his two sons. He now leads a group in Alpha similar to the one that helped him. He's sharing with others what Jesus has done for him. He's creating space to listen to people who feel far from God and show them that God is actually right here, inviting them to the party of his grace, peace, and purpose.

Transformed by Love

Remember Tom from the beginning of this chapter? Hair band rocker struggling with stage IV cancer and considering suicide? Tom received an incredible gift too. I asked him if he would give God a chance and he said "yes." Tom started attending our church. Many people in our church community "adopted" Tom. He belonged. We rallied together to provide for some of his medical expenses. We put together a meal train, a ride schedule for his doctor's visits, around-the-clock prayer, and even daily dog walking for his dogs. Tom saw the incredible love from a church community, and his heart started softening.

At one point, I told him, "Tom, your body might not be healed, but you can be free and full of peace through Jesus Christ." Tom prayed and became a Christian. He was filled with joy even in the face of impending death and difficulties in life.

One day we got a call; the top oncologist at one of the premier university hospitals in the country who works specifically with tongue cancer patients had heard of Tom through someone in our church. He invited Tom to his clinic for pro bono treatments. To this day, Tom is alive, cancer-free, smiling, drumming in church, serving God, and telling others of his love.

Go! Extend invitations to the party, share your story, listen with a heart of love, invite people to experience God's presence, leave judgment and correction out of it, and you will begin to live the greatest mission possible. You are part of his crew. You are the solution for a hurting world that needs the help of Jesus! It is more blessed to give than to receive and there is no greater gift than giving someone an introduction to the God who loves them.

CHAPTER 12

A Surprising Song

What is the deal about all the singing in church? Can we talk about that for a moment? I don't know about you, but I didn't expect to be joining the local congregational choir when I signed up to follow Jesus. After attending church for some time, I was still confused. "I get the value of meeting together with others, I get the value of listening to a message or sermon or homily or whatever you call it, I even get the value of giving and serving and getting involved. But why all the sing-alongs, why the Christian karaoke?" I thought.

Maybe you slayed a few solos in glee club when you were growing up (I may have dabbled in some high school musicals as Baby John in *West Side Story* and Jud Fry in *Oklahoma!* way back when, but I'm not admitting it here). Maybe you belt it out in the shower or at a Selena Gomez concert or sing your college anthem at kickoff. Or maybe you just stink at singing and never want to open your mouth when church songs start a strummin'. Whatever your melodic background, it seems following Jesus includes some songs, like, every single week—lots and lots of songs.

Before we finish our time together in this book, let's figure this one out. I've discovered it is far more foundational, poignant, and transformative than I first thought.

We are a fame-obsessed culture. How do I know? Because with four seconds of effort Cristiano Ronaldo can post a picture to 323 million followers of his luxury, pillow-top mattress installed in his initials-emblazoned private jet which happens to be the most expensive private jet sold to an individual in the world. In another two seconds, Katy Perry can show more than a hundred million people the new designer outfit she put on her dog Nugget. I'm not knocking Ronaldo and Katy (especially if you guys are reading this). I know they have problems too, and the glitz isn't all we think it is. Rather, I'm knocking our obsession with celebrity and fame.

If there is one truth about humanity, it's that we know how to worship. Why else do I know more details about Jay-Z's personal life than I know about my neighbor who lives two doors down the street? We can't help it. We worship. It's in our wiring. It's just a matter of what and whom we worship. It's critical to get this right because what we worship both reveals the state of our soul and determines the direction of our lives.

When I find myself lost in a celebrity binge—"What did they say, what did they eat, what did they buy now?"—I end up feeling hollow and trapped within the limits of my little life. As author Greg Beale said in his book by the same title, we become what we worship. If we worship striving for our own gain, we get emptiness because, as Jesus said, "We can gain the whole world yet lose our soul" (Matthew 16:26, my paraphrase). Our hearts have been pointed in the wrong direction.

You've probably heard the word "worship" associated with the church sing-along time. Or if you've paged through the book of Psalms, which I've mentioned earlier in this book, you'll realize it is a collection of "worship" songs as well as prayers. It is probably the first hymnal we know of. Take a look at these verses:

Come, let us bow down in worship, let us kneel before the LORD our Maker.

—Psalm 95:6

Let us come before him with thanksgiving and extol him with music and song. For the LORD is the great God, the great King above all gods.

—Psalm 95:2–3

Exalt the LORD our God and worship at his holy mountain, for the LORD our God is holy.

—Psalm 99:9

Worship the LORD with gladness; come before him with joyful songs.

—Psalm 100:2

This is just a sampling. The pages of Scripture are brimming with the concept of worshiping God. When you start to unpack all of it, you realize it isn't intended to be just a small add-on activity before the church announcements. Worship is the baseline of our existence. Like a tree always reaching toward the sunlight, we are designed to always reach toward the God of heaven in worship.

Why Worship?

Let's pause. For years, I couldn't really understand worship. I thought the whole following Jesus deal was about love. Why in the world would the loving God who redeemed me turn around and ask me to worship him? Isn't that complete arrogance or pride? I mean, that's what demagogues and dictators do: seek to be worshiped. Why would the God who calls me his beloved child, who wants a relationship with me, start telling me to praise him? That doesn't sound like a good father.

These questions stunted the growth of my heart. I was so put off by broken displays of power and pride in our world that I withheld worship from God.

Until I had a breakthrough. Sarah and I have an understanding. When her birthday comes, I must give her one thing. Presents are good, and yes, she wants them, but if we are in a financial bind, skip the presents, maybe even skip the party. But don't ever skip a handwritten card. Once I bought her a very nice present but forgot the handwritten card; it didn't go so well. Sarah's birthday card is a chance to tell her how much I love her and how thankful I am for our relationship. I've learned to go a little further now. I add affirmations about her characteristics that I most admire.

I say things such as, "Sarah, I appreciate your kindness; you are always there for your friends. I admire your perseverance; you don't give up when you know something is important. I respect how well you listen to me and others; we feel loved by you. You are gorgeous, I can't stop thinking about you . . ." Okay, enough of that.

Communicating this kind of admiration and praise, I noticed, actually rebounded back to me. The act of writing or speaking those words grew the affection in my heart for Sarah. Negativity has the same but opposing effect. If we speak and dwell on frustrations or say hurtful things about others, it compounds the negative view we carry toward those people. By speaking affirmations and praise, our love and respect grows, and it flows both from us and back to us. This could be one of the explanations behind worship. Literary giant and my writing hero, C. S. Lewis, points out:

> The most obvious fact about praise—whether of God or anything—strangely escaped me. I thought of it in terms of compliment, approval, or the giving of honour. I had never noticed that all enjoyment spontaneously overflows into praise . . . The world rings with praise—lovers praising their mistresses, readers their favourite poet, walkers praising the countryside, players praising their favourite game—praise of weather, wines, dishes, actors, motors, horses, colleges, countries, historical personages, children, flowers, mountains, rare stamps, rare beetles, even sometimes politicians or scholars. I had not noticed how the humblest, and at the same time most balanced and capacious, minds, praised most, while the cranks, misfits, and malcontents praised least . . . Except where intolerably adverse circumstances interfere, praise almost seems to be inner health made audible . . . I had not noticed either that just as men spontaneously praise whatever they value, so they spontaneously urge us to join them in praising it: "Isn't she lovely? Wasn't

it glorious? Don't you think that magnificent?" The Psalmists in telling everyone to praise God are doing what all men do when they speak of what they care about . . .

I think we delight to praise what we enjoy because the praise not merely expresses but completes the enjoyment; it is its appointed consummation. It is not out of compliment that lovers keep on telling one another how beautiful they are; the delight is incomplete till it is expressed . . . The Scotch catechism says that man's chief end is "to glorify God and enjoy Him forever." But we shall then know that these are the same thing. Fully to enjoy is to glorify. In commanding us to glorify Him, God is inviting us to enjoy Him.[1]

To enjoy God means that we experience the love, peace, fulfillment, truth, expansive pleasure of his presence and blessings and unconditional love in our lives. God knows that if we don't worship him, we are actually cutting ourselves off from his very presence—the enjoyment of himself. He is able to be more present in our lives the more we worship him. This is one reason God invites us to worship him—because, in worship, we experience more of him and grow in full enjoyment of him.

Another reason is rooted in the very definition of the word "worship." Worship means to acknowledge worth. That's why when we think of praising God and compare it to praising Aaron Rodgers, it's just silly. (It is always silly to praise anything connected to the Green Bay Packers, but that's not the point I'm trying to make here. No offense, my Cheesehead friends.)

Some of what we worship in this world has worth. A shiny new Tesla, a well-timed three-pointer, a singer or film director or professor or kind cashier. All have some worth, but none has all worth and none is perfect. We can't attribute human characteristics or behavior to God. We can't attribute human fallibility to him. In fact, there is nothing on this earth any of us have ever experienced before that compares to Christians worshiping God; it is a completely otherworldly concept.

All the worship and praise of cultural icons is like ash and dust compared to worshiping God. Worship of the created is a shadow compared to worshiping the Creator. All things, including people, are finite and are covered in tarnish. Yet, God has pure value and endless worth; he is incomparably great and unexplainably close. God is worthy of our worship unlike anything or anyone else.

Listen to the great worth of Jesus which the apostle Paul describes in Colossians 1. Hearing these words unlocks an innate response of worship in my soul.

> The Son is the image of the invisible God, the firstborn over all creation. For in him all things were created: things in heaven and on earth, visible and invisible, whether thrones or powers or rulers or authorities; all things have been created through him and for him. He is before all things, and in him all things hold together. And he is the head of the body, the church; he is the beginning and the firstborn from among the dead, so that in everything he might have the supremacy. For God was pleased to have all his fullness dwell in him, and through him to reconcile to himself all things, whether things on earth or things in heaven, by making peace through his blood, shed on the cross.
>
> **—Colossians 1:15–20**

When you first begin to worship God, it feels admittedly strange, incompatibly confusing with the rest of life and what we've known. Never have we praised something truly worthy of glory, until now.

And yet, there is an undercurrent beneath our worship which feels like the most natural, human, wired-into-our-very-being thing we have ever done. It's as if we were made to do this. Like a newborn clinging to its mother, we know worship of our good, loving, and powerful God is what we were intended to do. The most appropriate words I've ever spoken are words of worship to God. The most stirring songs I've ever sung are praise to my heavenly Father. You and I were designed to glorify him and, in that, we can enjoy him and his presence.

Here's the final reason for worship I'll mention. Worship is a compass. The magnetic pull and rotation of the earth always points a compass back to true north. (Unless you are stuck in Jules Verne's novel *Journey to the Center of the Earth*, then it points south!)

Remember the idolatry we discussed in chapter four, *Your Greatest Threat*? Idolatry is when we turn to the created to get what only the Creator can give. Ill-placed worship is giving to the created what only the Creator deserves. Idolatry and worship have an interconnected relationship. When we turn to some broken thing, our worship flows back out to broken things and we end up broken—a shipwrecked soul, disconnected from our true purpose. But when we turn to the Creator, our worship flows up to the Creator and we experience all enjoyment.

If you are wondering, "How's the health of my soul?" just look at your worship, and it will accurately tell you. Is praise of God flowing freely? Is his honor and the joy of his presence in your life pouring from your lips? If not, there's a broken connection.

Worship will always be the compass back to north, back to the way we were intended to be. Worship cuts off the process of idolatry and allows us to turn back to our good Creator to get what only he can give and to give what only he deserves. Worship is the way back home.

How to Worship

So, what do we do? Join the church choir? Well, sarcasm aside, yes, in a way. You and I are part of the chorus of this world. We join the angels, the sun and moon, the creatures in the sea, the waves crashing in, and with all people throughout all of time worshiping all that is good in the One and Only who is fully good. We get the privilege of singing this surprising song. You don't have to be in the actual church choir, but recognize you are already part of the heavenly one.

All of life is, or at least can be, worship. When you decide to give time or money to build God's kingdom instead of your own, that is worship. When you console a hurting friend in the name of the Lord, that is worship. When you open your Bible and let it shape you, that is worship. When you walk outside on a sunny day, taking in a deep breath, contented in every way, that is worship.

In fact, everything we've talked about in this book so far can be worship. Listening to the Holy Spirit, praying at all times and in all circumstances, reading and meditating on the Scripture. In each of these ways we are saying with our lives that God is worthy, that he deserves our attention, that he is the one we listen to and learn from and adore.

Surrendering our idols, coming out of hiding, staying at the table, forgiving and asking for forgiveness are all ways we worship. In these acts we align ourselves with God and say we delight in God more than we delight in our own ideas, individuality, rightness, or comfort. When we gather together in community and make choices that strengthen our connections, we are worshiping God with our lives through obedience to his greatest command—love God and love people.

Giving what God has entrusted to us, drawing near to those in need, and spreading the love of Christ can also be acts of worship. In these we declare that God is who he says he is, that he can provide so we don't have to cling to what we have, that he is close to the brokenhearted and needy, and that he loves us and others and longs for all to be saved. We worship the God who came close to us by coming close to others. We worship the God who gave to us by giving to others.

Worship is the great aim of our entire life. All personal growth in our faith and all outreach to this broken world is in fact grounded in and results in greater worship to our good Father in heaven. Nothing in our faith exists without worship.

On and on and on, we worship.

Yet, let's not let saying all things are worship become a way of avoiding the songs of worship. So, without creating or recreating some great debate, I'll restate Psalm 95:

> Let us come before him with thanksgiving
> and extol him with music and song.

> For the LORD is the great God,
> the great King above all gods.

—Psalm 95:2–3

We worship God in all things and in every way, but there is a reason every church in every context at every gathering sings songs of worship to God. Songs, the language of the heart, is the primary way we've been asked to worship God through Scripture. So, we sing.

Yes, we can and should sing on our own. You don't have to delete all of your non-Christian playlists in order to be in right relationship with God, but you'll find that worship music becomes more of the expression of your soul and you'll devote more and more of your time to it.

Yet it's not just singing songs on our own. It's singing songs *together* which makes up the biblical image of worship. Let "us" come before him; together, the Scripture says this is the picture we see of heaven, singing together. This is the image portrayed in the ancient people of God in the Old Testament. Songs, together. This is the account of the first church and the early church; persecuted, yet busting out in growth, and singing songs, together. Jesus reminds us again: "For where two or three gather in my name, there am I with them" (Matthew 18:20).

So, we sing, together, and the presence of God bursts forth from the songs of our hearts. It could be that times of individual worship are actually preparation for gathered, corporate worship within the local church. The people of God, coming together to receive and to grow, yes, but so much more than that. We gather together regularly and consistently to give to God what only he deserves, our worship. So, join a church, keep gathering, and stick with the church even when your church is imperfect and you are disillusioned. Worship him together.

Give him your best. Give him your all. Belt it out with abandon. Lift up your hands in joy. He made you. He's called you. He's saved you. He meets you in the dark. He points you toward the light. He redeems and restores you. He calls you his own. Sing. Sing together. Sing to the Lord. You were made for this.

Hallelujah!
Praise GOD from heaven,
    praise him from the mountaintops;
Praise him, all you his angels,
    praise him, all you his warriors,
Praise him, sun and moon,
    praise him, you morning stars;
Praise him, high heaven,
    praise him, heavenly rain clouds;
Praise, oh let them praise the name of GOD—
    he spoke the word, and there they were!

He set them in place
    from all time to eternity;
He gave his orders,
    and that's it!
. . .
Earth's kings and all races,
    leaders and important people,
Robust men and women in their prime,
    and yes, graybeards and little children.

Let them praise the name of GOD—
    it's the only Name worth praising.
His radiance exceeds anything in earth and sky;
    he's built a monument—his very own people!

Praise from all who love GOD!
    Israel's children, intimate friends of GOD.
Hallelujah!

—Psalm 148:1–6, 13–14 MSG

Let every living, breathing creature praise GOD!
   Hallelujah!

—Psalm 150:6 MSG

"You Got This"—A Note from Dad

My son Isaiah doesn't often openly share his inner world, but that day I knew he was feeling intimidated. I could see it on his long face and hear it through the deep sighs between sips of orange juice. He was solemn, a little moody, and dragging through breakfast. His world was changing; this was his first day of fourth grade at a brand-new school. You might know that same sensation—low-grade anxiety spilling into every artery as you stare down a mammoth challenge.

That's the impression I had after becoming a new Christian many years ago. It is true that we can have *simple* faith, but if anyone thinks living our faith is *easy*, that person is mistaken. Following Jesus is all-consuming. It is intended to be the central focus of our entire lives. It will hopefully be infused into every decision we make, every conversation we have, every thought which crosses our mind, and every action we take. You might be tempted, like me, to be overwhelmed. We need not be.

It was time to leave for school. Isaiah put his dishes in the sink, and I wrapped him in my arms and kissed him a few times on his forehead. I'm so glad that he still lets me do that. I handed him his lunch box and he hopped into the car with Sarah. He was off to face down the daunting day. Except he was equipped with a powerful weapon he didn't yet know about; earlier that morning I stuffed a short "dad note" into his lunch box:

"YOU GOT THIS. Much love, Dad"

I had complete confidence in him. I knew what kind of strength was in his little boy soul. I knew the kind of heart he had. I knew the amount of love and confidence he carried because of what Sarah and I had poured into him over the last decade. Besides that, if it didn't go well, I knew we would recover and regroup together.

Sure enough, at the end of the day, Isaiah came home full of energy, beaming, confident, and ready to go out to play. He broke through the initial barriers, started to make some friends, had some great interactions with his teacher. He overcame the fear and accomplished what seemed insurmountable. I didn't write that little note because I wanted to falsely prop him up. I said "you got this" because I knew deep down, he really had what it would take. And of course, I wrapped it in my love for him.

As you and I are peering into our future of following Jesus, we see all sorts of questions, difficulties, and areas where we may fail. Like a child starting out at a new school, we ask things like, "Will I be liked? Can I handle the workload? What if I mess up? What if this whole faith thing crumbles and I'm worse off because of it?"

We want our faith to last, we want to fall more in love with Jesus, we want to stay close to him, we want to receive all his blessings, we want to build his church, we want to make a significant difference in this broken world in his name. We don't want to let him or ourselves down along the way. But do we really have what it takes? Do you?

Thankfully, there are a few dad-notes in our lunch box too. Let these closing words sink in:

> Being confident of this, that he who began a good work in you will carry it on to completion until the day of Christ Jesus.
>
> **—Philippians 1:6**

> . . . And let us run with endurance the race that is set before us, looking to Jesus, the founder and perfecter of our faith. . . .
>
> **—Hebrews 12:1–2 ESV**

Let us hold unswervingly to the hope we profess, for he who promised is faithful.

—Hebrews 10:23

Do you see it?

You might be wondering whether you can really be faithful until the end. You, like me, might sometimes wonder if you have what it takes to fully follow Jesus.

The bad news is, I don't. You don't. On our own we do not have what it takes. But God says that doesn't matter; he is the one who started the good work in you, he is the author of your faith! And he is the one who will carry it on to completion, he is the perfecter of your faith! You can be hopeful because he is faithful. The faith you do have was designed by Jesus, it is in Jesus, for Jesus, refined by Jesus, and made complete by Jesus.

It doesn't matter how incomplete and imperfect you are. Your Father in heaven says, "You got this" because he knows what he has placed inside of you. You are bursting with his love. You are filled with his Spirit. He is covering you with his presence. He is calling you his own son or daughter. He is equipping you with spiritual gifts. He is speaking to you daily. He is going before and behind you. There is nowhere you can go where he isn't there for you. Your ally on this life changing, all-consuming, admittedly challenging journey is the very Creator himself. You are not on your own in this.

Nothing, the Scripture says, will be able to separate us from the love of God that is in Christ Jesus. As you keep your eyes fixed on Christ, you will endure. You will experience all that he is and become all he meant you to be. You can follow Jesus for the rest of your life. You can hold unswervingly, even imperfectly, on to him. You will endure with all the power and promise he has poured into your soul. You've got this because he's got you.

How to Begin Following Jesus

"Yet to all who did receive him, to those who believed in his name, he gave the right to become children of God."

—**John 1:12**

Beginning a relationship with Jesus is being adopted into the family of God. God is always, actively drawing us back to himself. He is the good Father working to bring those who feel far from him back into his family, back to his table of forgiveness and fulfillment.

Receiving Jesus is the starting line of a lifelong faith we've discussed throughout these chapters. If you feel stuck—somewhat empty or confused about whether you are his—it only requires a decision and a genuine prayer of your heart. Maybe it's time to take the words of John 1:12 as your own: "receive him . . . believe in his name . . . and become a child of God."

Sorry, Thank You, Please

It's a clear and simple prayer of saying "I'm sorry, thank you, and please"; like having a conversation with a dad we've walked out on. Follow along with me:

"I'M SORRY, *God, I've turned away from you and your ways all* *this time. I've done wrong and now I want that to end. I want to be yours. I choose for you to begin leading my life.*

THANK YOU, *Jesus, for dying on the cross. You paid the price for the wrongs I've done and taken my place. You rose from the dead so that, in you, I can rise from my death and separation from God now and for eternity.*

PLEASE, *Holy Spirit, come and fill me. I'm open to be led by you forever. I commit my life to you now, in Jesus' name."*

Wow. It may have been a short prayer, but history just split in two. From this moment on you are his. Nothing can ever change that. You can't undo this moment by living imperfectly; you can't improve upon it by achieving perfection. You are perfectly his, a child of God. Keep cultivating this new relationship like you would a garden: fertilize the ground, pull out the weeds, give it the light through the elements of faith we've discussed in this book.

Discussion Guide

Chapter 0: The Morning After

1. What's your story? How did you come to trust in Jesus?
2. Or, if you are still exploring faith, what has shaped your experience of Jesus up to this point in your life?
3. What has made your new or renewed faith difficult?
4. What has been something new you've discovered since you've trusted in Christ?

Chapter 1: Your Greatest Help

1. Have you sensed the Spirit guiding you in some way recently? Please describe. How did you respond?
2. Why is it sometimes challenging to "keep in step with the Spirit" for you?
3. In what ways have you experienced God's presence bringing you peace and reassuring you that you are not alone?
4. Have you ever experienced a miracle? What do you think is required for a miracle to occur?
5. Have you wanted to say or do something, and you sensed God saying "no" or "stop" as a way of protecting you?
6. What helps you take the way out of temptation when God provides it?
7. Is there a storm you are facing or a need you have for God's power to break through? Share it with the group and invite the Spirit of God to work in this area together.

Chapter 2: Your Greatest Skill

1. Share about a time in prayer when you felt deeply connected to God.
2. What does prayer look like throughout a normal week of your life right now?
3. What makes prayer difficult for you?
4. Take five minutes individually and write out your own CHAT prayer.
5. You don't need to share your prayer with the group, but talk about how you felt after that exercise.
6. What did you notice happened inside of you as you moved through the CHAT exercise?
7. What courageous prayer is it time for you to finally start praying?
8. What is a step of new intention toward prayer God is inviting you to take?

Chapter 3: Your Greatest Tool

1. Have you attempted to read parts of the Bible before? Was it helpful for you?
2. What has kept you from reading the Bible in the past?
3. Practice understanding the context. Pick a text to read together, maybe John 4:1–42, the woman at the well.
4. Try to answer the who, what, when, why of that passage. What insights can you glean together?
5. What time-transferable principle(s) rises to the surface for you as you study John 4:1–42?
6. Now, take some time on your own before sharing with the group. What way is God asking you to make this principle personal today?
7. What would it take for you to build a regular rhythm of 4Step Bible reading and reflection into your life?

Chapter 4: Your Greatest Threat

1. How do you tend to react when it doesn't look like God will come through for you?
2. Do you ever feel you need to earn God's love or repay him in any way?
3. Step one is to recognize the reality: If you had to name your version of a modern-day golden calf, what would it be? Achievement, people pleasing, standing out above the crowd, security for your future, or any other?
4. Step two is to reveal the root: What desire do you have that an idol may be trying to fulfill?
5. Step three is to find and fill the need: What would it look like for God to fill that desire for you?

Chapter 5: The First Response

1. Describe a lighthearted time when you may have attempted to hide something (a first date, a childhood memory, a "lost" assignment at school, etc.).
2. Why do you think our first reaction to something going wrong is often to hide or to cover it up?
3. What are some of the negative effects of withdrawing that you have either seen in others or experienced yourself?
4. What qualities do you think it takes for a Christian community to be life-giving and something you'd be willing to invest in?
5. Describe a time you have experienced some of those qualities from others.
6. Is there anything you might need to work through (a barrier, a fear, a bad past experience) in order to step effectively toward Christian community becoming a regular part of your life?
7. What is a first step you can try in order to create the community you long to experience for yourself?

Chapter 6: The Second Garden

1. The first and third gardens from the Bible (Eden and heaven) are pictures of perfection. Rattle off a few of the general aspects (in yourself or others) you can't wait to see changed in heaven. Note: This is not meant as an opportunity to get specific or talk about others in your group negatively.

2. What are some of your natural reactions when you see a behavior you don't like in another person? Examples: Do you keep it to yourself, do you confront the other person, do you pull back from them, do you put up a wall, etc.?

3. If you're willing to take a risk with the group, what is a plank or two you sometimes see in yourself that makes relationships difficult?

4. When Jesus came upon the man who was filled with greed and materialism, he looked at him and loved him. What does it take for you to see other people, flaws and all, and yet look at them and love them?

5. What makes it easier or more difficult to see beyond what is broken in others as Jesus did?

6. Applying the lens of grace to others is impossible to do unless we are applying the lens of grace to ourselves as well (love your neighbor as you love yourself). What is one specific area you can show yourself more grace?

7. From your perspective, what else is needed to be willing to stay at the table of a community filled with broken people?

8. What can help you persevere when you face disillusionment in Christian friendship?

Chapter 7: The Forgotten Step

1. Reflect on the common phrase, "Time heals all wounds." Do you agree? All or in part? Disagree? Why?

2. Reflect on the phrase, "Whatever doesn't kill you makes you stronger." Do you agree? All or in part? Disagree? Why?
3. Forgiveness means letting go of a debt; reconciliation means restoring the relationship. In what ways does it help you to separate the meanings of the two?
4. Do you think that true forgiveness can really happen without ever talking with the offending person? What makes that possible or impossible in your mind?
5. Do you think Christ's command to forgive is really for your own benefit? Why or why not?
6. Is there someone in your life whom you haven't forgiven (no need to share specifics)? What's your first step forward?

Chapter 8: The Final Flaw

1. Has anyone ever admitted their wrongdoing to you? How did it make you feel?
2. Do you think admitting where we've messed up benefits us? What do we gain through that process of honesty?
3. Which side of this statement is easier for you to do and why: confess to God for forgiveness or confess to others for healing?
4. Have you ever experienced what felt like a meaningless apology from someone? What made it feel that way?
5. Of the five steps in the apology crash course, which one or two most often stump you? Just a reminder, they are: express regret, accept responsibility, make restitution, genuinely repent, request forgiveness.
6. Just for fun, as a group turn to one another and say out loud three times, "I was wrong." Get that muscle working. Is there anyone out there after this discussion who could benefit from hearing those words from you?

Chapter 9: A Surprising Equation

1. What do you think was going through the disciples' heads when Jesus said, "You give them something to eat," and they handed Jesus just a few fish and loaves of bread?
2. What is difficult about embracing the concept that all we have is God's?
3. What helps provide perspective when you are feeling protective about your limited resources?
4. In what specific ways do you think God has been inviting you to be a coworker alongside him in accomplishing his work?
5. React to one another on the concept of tithing. What makes sense about it? What struggles do you have with it?
6. Have you ever seen a miracle in which God takes a little that someone gave and multiplied it into so much more? What happened? What impact did that have on you?
7. What is some natural resource in your life that God might be nudging you to release so that he can multiply it into a miracle?

Chapter 10: A Surprising Blessing

1. What was it like for you growing up in your socioeconomic background? How did that background shape you?
2. What makes it difficult to be close to people from different socioeconomic backgrounds than your own?
3. React to this statement: If you want to become more aware of God's presence in your life, increase your proximity to those in need.
4. What would have to change for you to increase your proximity to people in need?
5. Is there a resource in your life (time, energy, money, skills, connections, etc.) you think God has placed into your hands for the benefit of others?

6. What ideas do you have to let that flow through you to help another?

Chapter 11: A Surprising Mission

1. Talk about a time or two when you were more blessed in giving than in receiving.
2. Who helped you discover God's love and begin to follow Jesus? Talk about what they did that had a positive impact on you.
3. When someone asks you a difficult question about faith, how do you feel? How do you react?
4. What else keeps you from introducing people to the God who loves them?
5. What would help you increase your ability to share your faith?
6. Are there people in your life whom you'd love to see begin to follow Jesus? Spend extended time praying specifically for those people and for clear opportunities where you can take a next step in those relationships.

Chapter 12: A Surprising Song

1. How do you feel about singing out loud?
2. Do you try to worship God in any nonmusical ways throughout your day? If so, how?
3. When it comes to living out your new or renewed faith, in what areas do you feel the most confidence?
4. Where do you feel the least confidence?
5. How does realizing that God is both the author and perfecter of your faith help you?
6. What are the two or three major concepts from this book you have been able to apply to your life?
7. What one or two areas do you want to keep pressing in on to make more progress?

Notes

Chapter 2: Your Greatest Skill

1. This acronym is from the book *Prayer Coach* by Jim Nicodem (Wheaton, Ill.: Crossway Books, 2008).

Chapter 3: Your Greatest Tool

1. http://www.scripturaloutlines.org/believers/6b4.html. "The Word: Its Provisions Revealed through Metaphors," accessed September 4, 2019.

Chapter 4: Your Greatest Threat

1. N. T. Wright, *The Day the Revolution Began* (San Francisco: HarperOne, reprint edition, 2018).
2. Thomas Chalmers, *The Expulsive Power of a New Affection* (Minneapolis: Curiosmith, 2012).

Chapter 5: The First Response

1. Encyclopedia.com states that the term was coined by Joseph de Maistre around 1820 in France.

Chapter 6: The Second Garden

1. Dietrich Bonhoeffer, *Life Together* (San Francisco: HarperOne, 2009), page 27.
2. Parker J. Palmer, *On Staying at the Table: A Spirituality of Community*, n.p., n.d.

Chapter 7: The Forgotten Step

1. Anne Lamott, *Traveling Mercies: Some Thoughts on Faith* (New York: Anchor Books, 2000), page 200.
2. Pete Scazzero, *The Emotionally Healthy Church* (Grand Rapids, Mich.: Zondervan, 2010), page 10.
3. Brené Brown, *Rising Strong* (New York: Random House, 2017), page 156.

Chapter 8: The Final Flaw

1. Dr. Gary Chapman and Jennifer Thomas, *The Five Languages of Apology* (Chicago: Northfield Publishing, 2006).
2. Dr. John Townsend, *Hiding from Love* (Grand Rapids, Mich.: Zondervan, 1991).

Chapter 9: A Surprising Equation

1. http://www.preachingtoday.com/illustrations/1996/december/410.html.

Chapter 10: A Surprising Blessing

1. https://henrinouwen.org/meditation/meeting-god-poor/.

Chapter 11: A Surprising Mission

1. David Augsburger, *Caring Enough to Hear and Be Heard* (Ventura, Calif.: Regal Books, 1982), page 12.

Chapter 12: A Surprising Song

1. C. S. Lewis, *Reflections on the Psalms* (New York: Harcourt Press, 1958), pages 93–95.